To Phil, Lena
Best wishes.
Shriea

Laudato Si': AN IRISH RESPONSE

Laudato Si'
AN IRISH RESPONSE

Essays on the Pope's Letter
on the Environment

Edited by
Sean McDonagh

VERITAS

Published 2017 by
Veritas Publications
7–8 Lower Abbey Street
Dublin 1, Ireland
publications@veritas.ie
www.veritas.ie

ISBN 978 1 84730 749 1

10 9 8 7 6 5 4 3 2 1

Designed by Padraig McCormack, Veritas Publications
Printed in Ireland by SPRINT-print Ltd, Dublin

Veritas books are printed on paper made from the wood pulp of managed forests. For every tree felled, at least one tree is planted, thereby renewing natural resources.

Contents

INTRODUCTION
Laudato Si': A Prophetic Challenge for the Twenty-First Century
SEAN MCDONAGH 7

Anthropological and Theological Reflections on *Laudato Si'*
DERMOT A. LANE 31

Creation as Incarnation: Reflections on Biodiversity in *Laudato Si'*
JOHN FEEHAN 55

Laudato Si': Mining the Meanings for the City
MICHAEL PUNCH 83

The Disruptive Power of *Laudato Si'* – A 'Dangerous Book'
LORNA GOLD 91

Laudato Si' and Social Justice
BRIGID REYNOLDS AND SEÁN HEALY 105

Pope Francis on Power, Politics and the Techno-Economic
Paradigm
PEADAR KIRBY 125

Walking the Road from Paris
JOHN SWEENEY 137

From Vatican II to *Laudato Si'*
DONAL DORR 157

Demography, Poverty and Planetary Boundaries in *Laudato Si'*
CATHRIONA RUSSELL 173

LIST OF CONTRIBUTORS 197

Introduction:
Laudato Si': A Prophetic Challenge for the Twenty-First Century

SEAN MCDONAGH

The title of *Laudato Si'*, Pope Francis' encyclical on environmental and economic issues, is drawn from the opening words, 'Praised be to you'. These words, in the Umbrian dialect of St Francis of Assisi, are also the opening words of his wonderful 'Canticle of the Creatures', in which the saint gives thanks to God for the different creatures and other elements of creation: 'Brother Fire', 'Sister Moon' and 'Mother Earth' (87).

Pope Francis' encyclical is one of the most important documents to come from a pope in the past one hundred and twenty years – the era of modern Catholic social teaching. In this encyclical, the Pope wishes to address every person on the planet about the condition of our common home (3). He states quite bluntly that 'due to an ill-considered exploitation of nature, humanity runs the risk of destroying it and becoming in turn a victim of this degradation' (4). He uses quite startling language when he writes that 'the earth, our home, is beginning to look more and more like an immense pile of filth' (21). He then goes on to remind Christians 'that their responsibility within creation, and their duties towards nature and the Creator, are an essential part of their faith' (64). But he is adamant that there is 'an intimate relationship between the poor and the fragile planet' (16). He is convinced that 'a deep communion with the rest of nature cannot be real if our hearts lack tenderness, compassion and concern for fellow human beings'.

'Concern for the environment thus needs to be joined to a sincere love for our fellow human beings and an unwavering commitment to resolving the problems of society' (91). Pope Francis wishes that this document 'which is now added to the Church's social teaching, can help us to acknowledge the appeal, immensity and urgency of the challenge we face' (15).

Laudato Si' can be compared with three other crucially important social encyclicals. One dealt with the rights of workers, the second with the threat of nuclear war, and the third with the right to development for poor people.

Rerum Novarum ('New Things') by Pope Leo XIII in 1891 essentially inaugurated the era of modern Catholic social teaching. The teaching in this encyclical criticised the exploitation of workers, especially those working in factories (2). It called for a living wage and stated that workers had the right to form unions to protect themselves (36). The encyclical contradicted the central thesis of liberal capitalism that 'labour is a commodity to be bought at market prices determined by the laws of supply and demand rather than by the human needs of the workers (16–17, 33–34).[1]

In *Laudato Si'* Pope Francis refers to another historic encyclical, Pope John XXIII's *Pacem In Terris* ('Peace on Earth') written in 1963, 'when the world was teetering on the brink of the nuclear crisis' (3). That encyclical not only rejected war but provided a path to lasting peace.

Populorum Progressio ('The Development of Peoples'), which was written in 1967 by Pope Paul VI, created a framework for evaluating what kind of development could be called authentic human development. In the post-World War II era, there was significant economic growth in many countries in Europe, North America, Japan, and elsewhere. *Populorum Progressio*, however, did not give priority to economic development; rather it favoured development which is, 'for each and all, the transition from less human conditions to those which are more human' (20).

Previous Papal Teaching on the Environment

In *Laudato Si'* the Catholic Church takes on an even wider perspective, this time to embrace not just workers and the poor, but all creation as well. We will see that, although Pope Francis links his concern for the plight of the poor and the devastation of the earth to the teachings of his predecessors, there are many new insights in *Laudato Si'*. Naturally, as Bishop of Rome he would like to link his teaching to that of one of his predecessors. In *Laudato Si'* he recalls the warning that Pope Paul VI gave in a talk to the UN Food and Agriculture Organisation:

about the potential for an 'ecological catastrophe under the effective explosion of industrial civilization', and stressed the urgent need for a radical change in the conduct of humanity, in as much as the most extraordinary scientific advances, the most amazing technical abilities, the most astonishing economic growth, unless they are accompanied by authentic social and moral progress, will definitely turn against man. (4)

In his first encyclical, *Redemptor Hominis*, Pope John Paul II made the point that human beings frequently seem to 'see no other meaning in their natural environment than what serves immediate use and consumption' (5). In the same paragraph he went on to call for 'a global ecological conversion' (5). Pope John Paul II declared that action 'to improve our world entails profound changes in lifestyles, models of production and consumption, and the established structures of power which today govern society' (5). He also wrote an important document on ecology entitled *Peace with God the Creator, Peace with all Creation* on 1 January 1990. In this document he stated that 'the ecological crisis is a moral issue'. Ecological concerns appear in many of his encyclicals, especially in *Sollicitudo Rei Socialis* ('On Social Concerns'), written in 1987.

In *Laudato Si'* Pope Francis also calls to mind the work of his predecessor, Pope Benedict XVI, who, in his social encyclical *Caritas in Veritate*, asked people to 'recognise that the natural environment has been greatly damaged by our irresponsible behaviour and that the social environment has also suffered damage' (6). While these documents are insightful on social and economic issues, they remain decidedly human-centered, as if all the goods of the planet are meant just for human beings. *Laudato Si'* attempts to avoid this anthropocentric focus.

But *Laudato Si'* is the first papal document to understand the magnitude of the ecological destruction taking place globally and the urgency with which it must be faced. If you wish to get an idea of the extraordinary breakthrough in Catholic creation theology you just have to look at how it was dealt with in the *Compendium of the Social Doctrine of the Church*, which was published in 2014. The chapter devoted to 'safeguarding the environment' is only fifteen pages long, while the chapter on 'human work' runs to twenty-six pages. There is only half a paragraph devoted to climate change in that document (470) and the same is true for biodiversity (466), while there are nine paragraphs on biotechnology.[2] The book does not contain the sense of ecological crisis that is so evident in *Laudato Si'*.

Other Voices

One major change in Pope Francis' style as Bishop of Rome, that has enormous implications for ecclesiology, is that he is willing to include the voices of others, as he does in both his apostolic exhortation *Evangelii Gaudium* ('The Joy of the Gospel') and in *Laudato Si'*.

The first voice in *Laudato Si'* comes from the Ecumenical Patriarch Bartholomew, who since his election as patriarch in 1991, has constantly focussed on protecting God's creation, especially the water bodies of the world. Bartholomew focusses on the moral responsibility to protect creation when he writes that 'for human beings ... to destroy the biological diversity of God's creation; for human beings to degrade the integrity of the earth by causing changes in its climate, by stripping the earth of its natural forests or destroying its wetlands and its life – these are sins' (8). Subsequent to the publication of *Laudato Si'*, on 6 August 2015, the Feast of the Transfiguration, Pope Francis announced that he was selecting 1 September 2015 as a World Day of Peace for the Care of Creation. He called attention to the fact that the Orthodox Church, under the leadership of the Ecumenical Patriarch Bartholomew, already celebrated and prayed for creation on that day. The Pope believes that Christians from every tradition are now being called upon to offer their own contribution to overcoming the ecological crisis which is facing planet earth today. This is both a new spirituality and new moral teaching which previous generations of Christians did not have to deal with. For most of the two-thousand-year history of the Christian faith, moral teaching was focussed on human relationships with God and other human beings. Christians knew it was wrong to worship false gods, to kill, to steal, to commit adultery, or to lie. However, the majority of Christians never thought it was wrong to devastate forests or to drain marshes. Those who ploughed up the prairies of North American, or cut down the forests of Ireland, or used mercury for mining purposes in Australia, or devastated the tropical forests in the Philippines during the 1960s and 1970s, did not think of what they were doing as morally wrong. It is only during the past few decades that such actions have been considered sins. And even still, the majority of Catholics would not think of including such behaviour in their celebration of the Sacrament of Penance. So, if *Laudato Si'* is to have a profound, long-lasting influence on Catholic social and ecological teaching, it will need to be followed up with systematic and extensive moral catechesis.

Saint Francis of Assisi

Early on, Pope Francis acknowledges his devotion to St Francis, noting, 'I do not want to write this encyclical without turning to that attractive and compelling figure, whose name I took as my guide and inspiration when I was elected Bishop of Rome' (10). The Pope believes that 'Saint Francis is the example par excellence of care for the vulnerable and of an integral ecology lived out joyfully and authentically' (10). In the encyclical, the Pope is constantly emphasising the inseparable bond between concern for nature, justice for the poor, commitment to society, and interior peace (11), a bond exemplified by St Francis, who 'communed with all creation, even preaching to the flowers, inviting them "to praise the Lord," just as if they were endowed with reason' (11).

Anti-Body and Anti-Creature Sentiments

It would be nice to suppose that the vision of St Francis, especially his fraternal relationship with all creation, had continued and blossomed during the centuries after his death. Unfortunately, this did not happen. In fact, the opposite occurred; the creation-centred focus of St Francis' vision was lost, even among the Franciscans.

Sister Elizabeth Johnson places some of the blame with hierarchical dualism, which early Christian theology adopted in its encounter with the Hellenistic world that predated Francis by hundreds of year. Crucially she makes the point that 'this influential thought pattern not only sees the world in terms of the polarities of spirit and matter, but also prizes spirit as closer to the divine realm'.[3] She also claims that the late medieval distinction between natural and supernatural, designed to protect the gratuity of graces, focusses so much on the supernatural that 'it leached the presence and action of God on what was "merely" natural ... The world became no longer a gift but just a given, a background for the human drama.'[4]

This pessimistic, anti-world mood period was further strengthened by the extraordinary Europe-wide trauma of the Black Death (1346–53). This was one of the most devastating pandemics in human history. It claimed the lives of between seventy-five and two hundred million people, 30–60 per cent of Europe's population. Because of the speed of its transmission and the vast numbers of people affected, it sparked a series of religious, social and economic upheavals that had a profound effect on the course of European history. Clerical sermons in the wake of the plague interpreted it as a punishment from God. The only protection was to embrace a spirituality based on prayer, asceticism, mortification and a withdrawal from engagement with the world. Creation, as such, had no value.

Christians were warned not to be seduced by the allure of the world. Some aspects of the classic fifteenth-century text *The Imitation of Christ* by Thomas à Kempis illustrate this tendency. In a reflection, 'On Acknowledging Our Own Infirmities and the

Miseries of this Life', à Kempis writes, 'How, then, can this life be love, which is so full of bitterness and subject to so many trials? How can it be even called life since it brings forth so many deaths and spiritual plagues? Yet it is love and many seek all their pleasure in it.'[5] Sulpician Adolphe-Alfred Tanquerey, an early-twentieth-century spiritual writer, encouraged the novice to pray, 'May I know Thee, O Lord, and may I love Thee; May I know myself, that I may despise myself.'[6] Concern for creation was further diminished by the Reformation's almost exclusive focus on human salvation.

In an article in *The Furrow*, Patrick H. Daly calls attention to the advice that the great seventeenth-century preacher Jacques-Bénigne Bossuet, Bishop of Meaux (1627–1704) gave to those who flocked to hear his sermons. They were expected to exercise *mépris due monde*, distain for the world.[7] Daly believes this attitude helped fuel the modernist crisis and that it tarnished the posthumous reputation of Pius X.

The negative attitude to creation was also present in the missal of Pope Pius VI, which was used right up to the Second Vatican Council. The post-communion prayer during Advent read, *Domine, doceas nos terrena despicere, et amara celestia* ('Lord, teach us to despise the things of earth, and to love the things of heaven'). The same lack of appreciation for the beauty and value of creation is expressed in the prayer Salve Regina, which refers to the condition of human beings in this life as 'mourning and weeping in this valley of tears'. If our true home is in heaven and this world is just a valley of tears, all our energies need to be devoted to our interior life.

In the Catholic Church, Jansenism, an important theological movement in France in the seventeenth and eighteenth centuries, paid little attention to the importance of creation in the life of the believer. Their teaching focussed again on original sin, human depravity, the necessity of divine grace and predestination. Though condemned by Pope Clement IX and Pope Clement XI, ideas tinged with Jansenism made it difficult to highlight the revelatory aspect of creation.

With all these influences acting together, an anti-body/anti-other creature bias dominated the spiritual literature circulated in religious houses of formation right up to the time of the Second Vatican Council in the 1960s. Spirituality gave priority to the salvation of one's soul and the future life in heaven, rather than being involved in the affairs of the world.

This type of thinking was so prevalent in the Catholic Church that, as recently as 1961, Pope John XXIII had to remind Catholics in his encyclical *Mater et Magistra* that 'the laity must not suppose they would be acting prudently to lessen their Christian commitment to this passing world. On the contrary, we insist they must intensify it and increase it continually ... Let no one suppose that a life of activity in the world is incompatible with spiritual perfection' (254).

Of course, not everyone viewed creation in such a negative way. There were saints such as John of the Cross who felt that 'Mountains have heights and they are plentiful, vast, beautiful, graceful, bright and fragrant. The mountains are what my Beloved is to me.'[8]

But, such voices were exceptions. Many Christians, especially in the second millennium, had a much more jaundiced view and did not always respect the earth. Pope Francis acknowledges this: 'If a mistaken understanding of our own principles has at times led us to justify mistreating nature, to exercise tyranny over creation, to engage in war, injustice and acts of violence, we believers should acknowledge that by so doing we were not faithful to the treasures of wisdom which we have been called to protect and preserve' (200).

The Book of Genesis

In *Laudato Si'*, Pope Francis develops his own theology of creation. Many of the quotations are taken from the Bible and Pope Francis believes that 'our faith convictions can offer Christians, and some other believers as well, ample motivations to care for nature and the most vulnerable of brothers and sisters' (64). He begins by reviewing the creation stories from Genesis, finding there an affirmation of the goodness of the world, while also countering interpretations that are commonly invoked to justify a spirit of domination over nature.

The first chapter of the Book of Genesis tells us that the world was created by a loving, personal God. 'In the beginning God created the heavens and the earth' (Gn 1:1). The world is good in itself; God contemplates what he has done and found that 'it was good' (Gn 1:10, 13, 18, 21, 26). 'After the creation of man and woman, God saw everything that he had made, and behold it was very good' (Gn 1:31).

God's creative outpouring reaches its zenith in the creation of man and woman:

> Let us make man in our own image, in the likeness of ourselves, and let them be masters of the fish of the sea, the birds of heaven, the cattle, all the wild beasts and the reptiles that crawl upon the earth ... God blessed them, saying to them, 'Be fruitful, multiply, fill the earth and conquer it'. (Gn 1:26–8)

This command 'to fill the earth and conquer it' (Gn 1:28) has had a profound impact on the way Jews and Christians have related to the natural world. The New Jerusalem Bible uses the phrase, 'subdue it', while other translations say 'have dominion over it'. Pope Francis is aware that 'the Genesis account which grants "dominion" over the earth, has encouraged the unbridled exploitation of nature by painting humankind as domineering and destructive by nature' (67). The Pope is adamant that 'this is not a correct interpretation of the Bible as understood by the Church' (67).

In the second account of creation the Pope points out that in Genesis 2:15, God commands Adam and Eve to 'till and keep' the garden of the world (Gn 2:15). '"Tilling" refers to cultivating, ploughing or working while "keeping" means, caring, protecting, overseeing and preserving' (67). As far as the Pope is concerned, this text calls on humans to be thoughtful and careful in the way they relate to creation, though he does admit that 'it is true that we Christians have at times incorrectly interpreted the Scriptures, nowadays we must forcefully reject the notion that being created in God's image and given dominion over the earth justifies absolute dominion over other creatures' (67).

Pope Francis joins modern biblical scholars who insist that the divine command in Genesis 1:28 cannot be interpreted as a licence for humans to change and transform the natural world according to any human whim or fancy. The dominion given in Genesis 1:28 is, in fact, a challenge to human beings to imitate God's loving kindness and faithfulness and to act as his viceroy in relationship with the non-human component of the earth.

Like viceroys of the king, men and women were expected to be just and honest and to render real service. They were forbidden from exploiting the people or the earth. Furthermore, exegetes remind us that the first account of creation does not end at Genesis 1:31 with the creation of humans: it ends rather in Genesis 2:3 with the Sabbath rest of God. The Sabbath was a very important institution for the people of Israel, both for the well-being of humans and other creatures. Pope Francis highlights the importance of the Sabbath, as a time of rest for everyone, and the Jubilee, as a way of distributing the goods of creation (71).

Genesis Understood from the Sixteenth to the Nineteenth Century

The Pope rejects any understanding of word 'dominion' that would devalue creation and give humans tyrannical control over it. Although contemporary scripture scholars agree with the Pope, this argument faces an uphill battle against centuries of interpretation to the contrary. In Tudor and Stuart England, for example, the biblical teaching on 'dominion' over creation was interpreted in just this way. As Keith Thomas notes in his book *Man and the Natural World: A History of the Modern Sensibility,* the Bible taught that:

> **the world had been created for man's sake and that other species were meant to be subordinate to his wishes and needs ... those theologians and intellectuals who felt the need to justify it could readily appeal to the classical philosophers and the Bible. Nature made nothing in vain, said Aristotle, and everything had a purpose. Plants were created for the sake of animals and animals for the sake of man. Domestic animals were there to labour, and wild ones to be hunted. The Stoics had taught the same: nature existed solely to serve man's interests.[9]**

This anthropocentric and mechanistic vision of creation was, of course, not confined to people like Francis Bacon (1561–1626) and Isaac Newton (1642–1727) in Britain. The French philosopher René Descartes (1596–1650) believed that 'man stood to animal as did heaven to earth, soil to body, culture to nature. There was a total qualitative difference between man and nature.'[10] Aware of this history, Pope Francis points out that 'unhealthy dualism, nonetheless, left a mark on certain Christian thinkers in the course of history and (as a result) disfigured the Gospel' (98). The tragedy for the world is that this human-centred and dualistic approach to nature was firmly in place at the beginning of the scientific and technological era when James Watt was experimenting with his steam engine in 1750. Robin McKie, science editor of *The Observer*, argues that 'today, many scientists believe that the processes unleashed by Watt have begun to alter the physical make up of our planet. After two-and-a-half centuries of spewing out carbon dioxide from power plants and factories built in the wake of the condenser's invention, the atmosphere and crust of the earth are beginning to be transformed. Watt truly changed the world, it seems.'[11]

When *Laudato Si'* was published on 24 May 2015, many people turned immediately to look at what the document had to say about climate change. Pope Francis was clear and unambiguous, 'A very solid scientific consensus indicates that we are presently witnessing a disturbing warming of the climate system' (23). Further down in that paragraph, the text claims that humans are mainly responsible for releasing the greenhouse gases that cause climate change into the atmosphere. So, in one paragraph Pope Francis makes it clear that he accepts the scientific consensus that climate change is happening and that humans are generating the greenhouse gases that are causing the change. The focus on climate change led some people to think that this was the only theme discussed in the encyclical. In fact, the encyclical also deals with poverty, the destruction of biodiversity, the pollution of fresh water and the oceans, sustainable food, extractive industries and the waste created by the global economy. At a two-day meeting on 'People and the Planet First: The Imperative To Change' (2–3 July 2015) sponsored by the Pontifical Council for Justice and Peace and CIDSE, Cardinal Turkson said on a number of occasions that the encyclical was about much more than climate change.

In the past, the Catholic Church has not always spoken out emphatically on the issue of climate change, especially during the 1980s and 1990s when the voice of the World Council of Churches (WCC) was much louder. The Catholic Church's voice was quite mute during the 1990s and in the first decade of the twenty-first century when the climate change debate began; the Intergovernmental Panel on Climate Change (IPCCC), established in 1987, and groups such as the World Council of Churches were more engaged and vocal about ecological issues. The WCC published an excellent document on climate in 1994 called *Accelerated Climate Change: Sign of Peril, Test of Faith.*[12] Back in 1993, the researchers accepted scientific evidence for climate change and attempted to predict what the consequence would be. They also helped develop a theological and ethical framework to help Christians to understand the implications of climate change for their faith. Recommendations were made to countries, corporations and individuals to reduce their greenhouse gas emissions. It examined the potential role of the churches in addressing the crisis of human-induced climate change. The document focussed on the prophetic vocation of the churches to denounce evil and to seek ways to reduce greenhouse gas emissions and to work creatively with secular organisations, such as the Friends of the Earth. I was part of a group which included other Catholics who worked with the committee which drew up this document.

Pontifical Council's Conference on Climate Change

In May 2007, the Pontifical Council for Justice and Peace organised a two-day seminar on climate change. Over eighty people attended. While there were excellent presentations from credible scientists, whose writings had been peer reviewed, incredibly the organisers gave a platform to at least four participants who either denied the existence of climate change or who believed it was a good thing. One of these was Professor Craig Idso, adjunct professor at the

Office of Climatology at Arizona State University (ACU). He is chairman of the Center for the Study of Carbon Dioxide and Global Change, an institute which is dedicated to denying climate change. Together with his father, Sherwood, and his brother, Keith, he co-authored a report entitled 'Enhanced or Impaired? Human Health in a CO_2-enriched world', which argues that global warming and an increase in atmospheric CO_2 would be beneficial to humanity. ExxonMobile states on its website under the heading of 'Community Development' that it gave $6.2 million in 2006 to fund public information and public policy institutes. Idso's Center is listed as having received $10,000.

Why did the Pontifical Council for Justice and Peace give so much prominence to these contrarians? Is it because they mistakenly thought that there was still significant doubt about the science underpinning climate change, despite the testimony of the IPCC? Naomi Oreskes, a scientist at the University of California, analysed nine hundred and twenty-three articles in scientific journals written between 1993 and 2003. She published the results of her findings in *Science* in December 2004. Not a single scientific article disputed that human activity was causing a rise in global temperatures. These conclusions have also been endorsed by leading scientific organisations around the world, including the Science Academies of Brazil, India and China.

Climate change was not mentioned in Pope Benedict's encyclical *Caritas in Veritate* (Love in Truth), which was published just a few months before the United Nations Framework Convention in Copenhagen in December 2009. The Irish Jesuit and scientist Fr John Moore wrote an article entitled '*Caritas in Veritate:* An Ecological Perspective', saying that, 'for this reason, I find that Pope Benedict's treatment of ecology in his recent encyclical *Caritas in Veritate* and in his letter for 2010 World Peace Day ... so satisfying. He avoids any reference to the currently "fashionable" demands for reduction in carbon dioxide and keeps clear of the "doomsday" predictions about global warming and the future of the planet.'[13] That article was written just six years ago, showing just how revolutionary the clear statement in *Laudato Si'* that affirms climate change is happening and that humans are mainly responsible for it actually is.

This ambivalence changed dramatically with the publication of *Laudato Si'*. Pope Francis states, 'The climate is a common good, belonging to all and meant for all ... a very solid scientific consensus indicates that we are presently witnessing a disturbing warming of the climatic system. In recent decades this warming has been accompanied by a constant rise in the sea level, and it would appear, by the increase of extreme weather events, even if a scientifically determinable cause cannot be assigned to each particular phenomenon' (23). The Pope names the gases involved in climate change. 'Scientific studies indicate that most global warming in recent decades is due to the great concentration of greenhouse gases (carbon dioxide, methane, nitrogen oxides and others)' (23). He then links this to the 'model of development based on the intensive use of fossil fuel' (23). The central theme of the encyclical, which links the plight of the poor and the care of earth, is taken up here as well when Pope Francis claims that the 'worst impact [of climate change] will be felt by developing countries in coming decades' (25). The Pope states that 'The warming caused by huge consumption on the part of some rich countries has repercussions on the poorest areas of the world, especially Africa where a rise in temperature, together with drought, has proved devastating for farming' (51). Pope Francis reminds us that we have obligations to the poor and to future generations when he writes that 'twenty percent of the world's population consumes resources at a rate that robs the poor nations and future generations of what they need to survive' (96). Pope Francis is also convinced that fossil fuel products

– coal, oil and gas – cannot continue to be the dominant source of energy for our global economy.

According to many scientists the earth is experiencing the sixth greatest extinction of life since life began 3.8 billion years ago.[14] Pope Francis puts it more graphically 'the earth's resources are being plundered because of short-sighted approaches to the economy, commerce and production' (34). What is now happening is comparable to the extinction event which wiped out the dinosaurs as well as almost half the species of the world sixty-five million years ago. Though there is still some uncertainty among paleontologists as to the cause of the extinction, the major factor in this event was a ten-kilometre asteroid which struck what is now the Yucatán peninsula in Mexico. The effect was global. Forest fires burned around the world. These blocked out sunlight and led to a cold period.

Pope Francis realises that this current mass extinction is a direct result of human activity on the planet (33). The extinction rate in the twentieth century is up to one hundred times higher than it would have been without human activity.[15] Dr Gerardo Ceballos of the National Autonomous University of Mexico said that this is a conservative study 'which only looked at species that had been declared extinct'.[16]

This is why the emeritus professor of biology in Harvard University, Dr Edward Wilson, wrote in the year 2000 that the 'quenching of life's exuberance will be more consequential to humanity than all present day warming, ozone depletion and pollution combined'.[17] He is not the only person sounding the alarm. A study by the International Union for the Conservation of Nature (IUCN), conducted in 2010, estimates that one in five mammals, one in four plants, one in three amphibians and one in eight birds are in danger of being pushed over the precipice of extinction.[18] David Roberts, from the Durrell Institute of Conservation and

Ecology at the University of Kent, one of the co-authors of the study, said that 'if we take the number of species that are known to be threatened, and add to that those that are yet to be discovered, we can estimate that between 27 per cent and 33 per cent of all flowering plants will be threatened with extinction'.[19] The paper makes the point that these are conservative projections and do not take account of the number of species which will become extinct because of global warming.

In *Laudato Si'*, Pope Francis discussed the destruction of species. He laments the fact that 'the loss of forests and woodlands entail the loss of species which may constitute extremely important resources in the future, not only for food but also for curing disease and other uses. Different species contain genes which could be key resources in years ahead for meeting human needs and regulating environmental problems' (32).

By wilfully destroying biodiversity human beings ignore the fact that all creatures have 'intrinsic value in themselves independent of their usefulness. As Pope Francis points out, each organism, as a creature of God, is good and admirable in itself; the same is true of the harmonious ensemble of organisms existing in a defined space and functioning as a system' (140).

This is certainly new teaching and it has enormous implications for Christians living in our world today. If each species has intrinsic value, we humans are challenged to be attentive to them and their habitat, so that humans and all other creatures can thrive on earth. Seldom do modern humans show the kind of empathy towards nature that was so typical of St Francis of Assisi. We pay little attention to trees or flowers around us and we rarely allow nature to evoke any type of emotional response from us.

Increasingly, modern technology is widening the gap between ourselves and the rest of creation. This is partly because so few of us plant and harvest the food we eat, nor do we live in close contact with nature. Just think of the amount of time people spend on their iPads or mobile phones instead of getting to know, appreciate and love creation!

If we took the intrinsic value of creation seriously, we would be imitating what Adam did in the Garden of Eden. He was asked by God to name all the creatures in his world (Gn 2:19–20). We should be as knowledgeable about our world as he was about his. This would mean learning the names of the birds, the insects, the trees, the creatures of the oceans, the wild flowers and mosses and the grasses in our locality. This kind of attentiveness to creation would become the foundation stone of our creation spirituality.

Since nature and technology move at a very different pace, this kind of active rootedness in our local place would slow us down, removing us from what Pope Francis calls 'rapidification' and allowing us to enter into a fuller relationship with creation and with God (18).

From this perspective, protecting biodiversity should be one of the primary goals of human life, the central human vocation. Pope Francis tells us that ecological conversion 'also entails a loving awareness that we are not disconnected from the rest of creatures, but joined in a splendid communion' (220).

The Conference of the Parties to the UN Convention on Biodiversity, which Pope Francis mentions (167), has received very little media coverage over the years, unlike the similar convention for climate change. In 2010, at the opening ceremony, Ahmed Djoghlaf, Executive Secretary of the Convention on Biological Diversity, told the sixteen thousand participants who had gathered from across the world that they are called to seriously address the unprecedented loss of biodiversity that is further compounded by global warming. He stated that 'if we allow current trends to continue we shall soon reach a tipping point with irreversible and irreparable damage to the capacity of the planet to sustain life on earth. The report warns that the status of biodiversity for the next million years will be determined by the action or inaction, of one species – human beings.'[20] The Catholic Church, which presents itself as a pro-life Church, should take a special interest in the UN Convention on Biodiversity.

In *Laudato Si'*, Pope Francis states that his message about environmental deterioration is addressed to 'all men and women of good will' (3). He notes that every effort to protect and improve our world entails profound changes in 'lifestyles, models of production and consumption' (5). Pope Francis is not overwhelmed by the sheer magnitude of the ecological crisis because he believes that 'things can change' (13). He is adamant that 'young people demand change … they wonder how anyone can claim to be building a better future without thinking of the environmental crisis and the sufferings of the excluded' (13). Of course, Pope Francis realises that 'change is impossible without motivation and a process of education' (15). He notes that some progress is being made. 'Investments have also been made in means of production and transportation which consume less energy and require fewer raw materials, as well as in methods of construction and renovating buildings which improve their energy efficiency. But these good practices are still far from widespread' (26).

As I read this section of *Laudato Si'*, I asked myself, will this transformative education happen? Will humans turn from being 'masters, consumers [and] ruthless exploiters' to feeling 'intimately united to all that exists' (11)? As someone who has been involved in environmental theology in the Philippines and Ireland for almost forty years, I am convinced that without serious reflection and education at an individual and community level *Laudato Si'* will be ineffective, because what is called for here will involve massive changes.

Without Extensive Education, Nothing will Happen

I am reminded that twenty-seven years ago in January 1990, Pope John Paul II published a document on ecology entitled, 'Peace with God the Creator: Peace with all of Creation'. In its first paragraph, that document stated that 'in our day there is a growing awareness that world peace is threatened … by a lack of due respect for nature [and] by the plundering of natural resources.' Pope John Paul II ends that first paragraph with the words, 'Moreover, a new ecological awareness is beginning to emerge which, rather than being downplayed, ought to be encouraged to develop into concrete programs and initiatives.' He states that 'an education in ecological responsibility is urgent: responsibility for oneself, for others, and for the earth' (13). He claims that 'Christians, in particular, realise that their responsibility within creation and their duty towards nature and the Creator are an essential part of their faith. As a result, they are conscious of a vast field of ecumenical and interreligious cooperation opening up before them' (15). Unfortunately, this vision of Pope John Paul II failed miserably. Very few Catholic communities embraced the task of working to protect the poor and the embattled earth. The document called for a 'more internationally coordinated approach to the management of the earth's goods' (9). This also has not happened, because resources were not committed to making it happen.

A Three Year Synod on Ecology at Local, National and International Level

One way the Church could begin educating itself about these issues is through a synodal process. A synod is a council of the Church, usually convened to make decisions on doctrine or issues considered important by the Church at a particular time. So, given the importance of working for the poor and protecting the environment, as highlighted in *Laudato Si'*, it would make a lot of sense to hold a synod on these topics. The synod should run for at least three years. The first year might be spent getting to know the local environment in each parish and diocese. What are the ecosystems in the area and how are they being impacted in recent times? Obviously, people with knowledge and skills in this area could be called to share their expertise with the members of the synod, most of whom would be lay people. It would be important that there be a good age mix at the synod; older and younger people should be encouraged to take part.

The synod could begin to engage with the questions that Pope Francis has raised in *Laudato Si'*. In terms of climate change, for example, the synod would discuss the level of greenhouse gas emissions in that area from either transport or agriculture and suggest various ways to reduce these emissions quickly. In some synods this might raise difficult issues; for example, in Ireland it may call into the question the morality of our heavy meat diet, not just because of its impact on the local environment but on the planet as well. Our diet must change significantly because it contributes to global warming, and this will only happen through robust debate and dialogue. Naturally, if these changes are to take root, profitable farming alternatives would have to be suggested and supported in order to sustain the farming community in the area.

Similar issues will emerge in terms of our use of energy, water use and waste. The synod would also attempt to develop a spirituality which will make it easier for local Catholic groups to honour their relationship with God, with fellow humans, with other creatures and the natural world. Appropriate liturgies could also be suggested and developed as the synod members were trying to tease out what this new, more harmonious way of living might entail. For the second year of the synod, a similar process should take place at national level and, in the third year, an international synod could be held. This would be a huge boost to ecological thinking and action around the world and the Catholic Church could play a vital role as a catalyst facilitating the whole process.

Endnotes

1. Cited in Donal Dorr, *Option for the Poor and the Earth: Catholic Social Teaching*, New York, Orbis Books, 2012, p. 19.

2. *Compendium of the Social Doctrine of the Church*, 2004, Dublin: Veritas, pp. 213–28.

3. Elizabeth A. Johnson, 'Is God's Charity Broad Enough for Bears?', *The Irish Theological Quarterly*, 2015, p. 284.

4. Ibid.

5. Thomas à Kempis (ed.), Clarke L. Fitzpatrick, *The Imitation of Christ*, New York: Catholic Book Publishing Co., p. 141.

6. Quoted in Matthew Fox, *Original Blessing*, Santa Fe: Bear and Company, 1983, p. 59.

7. Patrick H. Daly, 'Voice of the Bishop in the Public Square', *The Furrow*, p. 140.

8. Taken from Cardinal Cahal Daly, *The Minding of Planet Earth*, Dublin: Veritas, 2004, p. 55.

9. Keith Thomas, *Man and the Natural World: A History of the Modern Sensibility*, New York: Pantheon Books, 1983, p. 17.

10. Ibid., p. 35.

11. Robin McKie, 'Water, Steam and the Sabbath Stroll that Sparked the Industrial Revolution', *The Observer*, 24 May 2015, p. 32.

12. WCC, *Accelerated Climate Change: Sign of Peril, Test of Faith*, 1993.

13. John Moore SJ, *Caritas in Veritate*: An Ecological Perspective', *JCTR Bulletin*, 85, 2010, pp. 23–4.

14. Adam Vaughan, 'Earth Heading for Sixth Mass Extinction', *The Guardian*, 20 June 2015, p. 9.

15. Ibid.

16. Ibid.

17. Edward O. Wilson, 'Vanishing Before Our Eyes', *Time Special Edition*, April/May 2000, p. 30.

18. Juliette Jowit, 'At Least a Quarter of Flowers May Face Extinction,' *The Guardian*, 7 July 2010, p. 5.

19. Ibid.

20. 'Statement by Ahmed Djoghlay Executive Secretary of the Convention on Biological Diversity at the Opening Session of the Tenth Meeting of the Conference of the Parties to the Convention on Biological Diversity', 18 October 2010, cbd.int/doc/speech/2010/sp-2010-10-18-cop10-en.pd

Anthropological and Theological Reflections on *Laudato Si'*

DERMOT A. LANE

The publication of the papal encyclical *Laudato Si': On the Care for Our Common Home* has created a stir in secular and religious circles. The encyclical is addressed to the whole of humanity, and not just Christians or Catholics. It has been described as a prophetic document, calling for nothing less than 'a cultural revolution' and an ecological conversion for all (114).

The encyclical was published in May 2015. It has received a positive reception from scientists and religious people alike. It was well received by the *Islamic Declaration on Global Climate Change* (Istanbul, August 2015) and by a Jewish response from US rabbis in summer 2015. In December 2015, the UN Climate Change Conference, Paris spoke well of the encyclical. In April 2016, the *Interfaith Statement on Climate Change* was published to coincide with a UN signing ceremony endorsing the UN 2015 Paris Agreement in New York on Earth Day, April 2016.

The encyclical belongs to the genre of Catholic Social Teaching that began with the publication of *Rerum Novarum* some one hundred and twenty-five years ago. That encyclical by Leo XIII was the Church's response to the economic changes taking place during and after the Industrial Revolution. This new encyclical is the Church's response to the global ecological crisis afflicting the twenty-first century. Francis builds on statements made by his papal predecessors, such as Paul VI, John Paul II and Benedict XVI, indicating that what he is saying is in continuity with his predecessors. But equally important he goes beyond previous popes: offering an analysis of what is happening to our common home in chapter one; drawing on the wisdom of the Bible and the Christian tradition in chapter two; outlining the roots of the ecological crisis in chapter three; developing what he calls an 'integral ecology' in chapter four; calling for a global dialogue on the environment in chapter five; proposing a programme of ecological education and spirituality leading to ecological conversion in chapter six.

Most of the commentary on *Laudato Si'* has been about the huge moral questions raised by the encyclical:

- The critique of unfettered capitalism.
- A call to hear the cry of the earth *and* the poor as linked.
- An acknowledgement that climate change affects the poor most.
- The importance of solidarity between the developing world and the so-called developed world.
- The centrality of solidarity between humans and the natural world.
- The promotion of not only social justice but also climate justice between the nations and between the generations (159–62).
- The development of what Pope Francis calls 'intergenerational solidarity' (159), asking: 'What kind of world do we want to leave to those who come after us?' (160) and then answering rather

bluntly: 'We may well be leaving to the coming generations debris, desolation and filth' (161).

These are some of the key ethical issues at the centre of the encyclical. Instead of addressing these particular questions I wish to take a different approach. I want to discuss the anthropological and theological foundations that inform the encyclical. These foundations are not to the fore in the document. They do exist, but only scattered throughout the encyclical. Further, I want to locate these foundations within the context of what contemporary science tells us about the history of the universe. We cannot deal then with ecology without taking account of what is going on in science. This brief theological commentary on *Laudato Si'* seeks to do three things:

1. Discuss the importance of the dialogue between religion and science as context.
2. Outline some of the anthropological challenges facing humanity in the twenty-first century.
3. Sketch some of the pneumatological and Christological foundations behind *Laudato Si'*.

The Dialogue between Religion and Science

Francis recommends an *intense* and *fruitful* dialogue between religion and science (62). Science is an important part of the context for developing an ecological theology, especially what is called the science of cosmology, which outlines the history of the cosmos and the science of evolution concerned with the biological history of humanity.

For a long time, there has been a stand-off between Christianity and science. We have the sorry story of Galileo who was condemned by the Church. Subsequently, there has been a suspicion surrounding science, and in particular around Charles Darwin's theory of evolution.

In recent times, however, and particularly in the last fifty to sixty years, there has been a new and productive dialogue between religion and science. There is a growing realisation that religion and science, while distinct, can enhance each other. Thus, John Paul II, in 1988, suggested: 'Science can purify religion from error and superstition; religion can purify science from idolatry and false absolutism.'[1] Later, John-Paul II acknowledged that evolution is more than just a hypothesis.[2]

We live in a world today in which the findings of contemporary cosmology and theories of evolution are accepted broadly as part of the fabric of life. This scientific outlook on the world provides context for approaching this encyclical and developing its anthropological and theological foundations. We cannot do theology with our backs to science.

Contemporary cosmology charts a history of the universe that goes back some 13.7 billion years. Scientists talk about a Big Bang at the origins of the universe, and describe this event as a singular explosion with an extraordinary expansion of energy. In the light of this new cosmic story, scientists make a number of observations about the intricate relationship that exists between the different stages of cosmology. Firstly, it is pointed out that we live in a finely tuned universe; for example, the well-known Stephen Hawking observes in his book *A Brief History of Time* that: 'If the rate of expansion of one second after the Big Bang had been smaller, by even one part of a hundred thousand million, the universe would have re-collapsed before it reached its present size.'[3]

Secondly, some scientists hold that the universe evolved in the particular way it did because it was programmed or coded to support life. This is sometimes known as the Anthropic Principle, a principle which holds that the universe is wired in some sense to support human existence. These observations help us to understand Francis' emphasis throughout the encyclical that everything is interconnected, interrelated and interdependent. On the other hand, believers must be careful not to rush in with theological explanations for what was happening in the Big Bang. The Big Bang is a scientific theory outside the competence of theology; for example, to suggest that God caused the Big Bang is open to misunderstanding. Instead, theology depends on Revelation for its understanding of God, and not Science as such.

A third implication of this new cosmic story is the discovery of an intimate relationship between human beings and the earth. Scientists are now talking about human beings as cosmic dust in a state of consciousness. In an important sense, the human is the culmination of the unfolding history of the cosmos and the evolution of life on earth. We need the human to understand the story of the cosmos, but equally we need the story of the cosmos to understand who the human is.

This new cosmic story opens up vast perspectives on the universe in which we live and on our place within the earth community and the human community. It is possible to discern a line of development from cosmic origins to our present self-understanding in the following sweep: Big Bang; energy; stars; matter; molecules; earth; biological life; human life; consciousness; self-consciousness; reflective self-consciousness; historical consciousness; global consciousness; freedom and responsibility; care and compassion; solidarity; a call to universal communion within diversity.

A fourth implication of the new cosmic story is that we must move out of the Newtonian universe; a mechanistic understanding of the world, seeing it as made up of bits and pieces of matter than can be broken down into isolated and disconnected atomic parts. It was in the context of the Newtonian paradigm that the breakdown of the unity between God, human beings and the earth took place, and this, in turn, led to the emergence of a disenchanted universe. Within a disenchanted universe there followed the dislocation of the human from community and the emergence of the self-sufficient subject of modernity. In the light of this dialogue between science and religion, and, in particular, in the context of the new cosmic story we can now look at anthropology as one of the sources of the ecological crisis, as well as one of the solutions to this crisis.

Anthropological Issues For The Twenty-First Century

The Critique of Anthropocentrism in *Laudato Si'*

One of the underlying themes within the encyclical is anthropology. Francis points out:

> **Many things have to change course, but it is we human beings above all who need to change. We lack an awareness of our common origin, of our mutual belonging, of a future to be shared with everyone. (202)**

No amount of talk about ecology will succeed unless and until we come up with what he calls 'a new way of thinking about human beings' (215).

The modern understanding of 'man' is a major part of the ecological crisis.[4] As Francis points out, 'There can be no ecology without an adequate anthropology' (118).

This is a first principle in the encyclical. *Laudato Si'* puts up in red lights what it calls the 'crisis and effects of modern anthropocentrism'. It critiques what it calls 'tyrannical' (68), 'distorted' (69) and 'misguided' (118, 119, 122) expressions of anthropocentrism. These are strong adjectives and leave no room for ambiguity. By anthropocentrism Francis means an outlook that puts man at the centre of the universe, making the human the measure of all things and, therefore, subordinating everything to serve the needs of man.

According to the encyclical, 'modernity has been marked by an excessive anthropocentrism' (116) and this anthropocentrism has compromised the intrinsic dignity of the natural world (115). A causal connection is made between the self-understanding of modern man and the damaged dignity of the natural world. Francis observes, 'Once the human being declares independence from reality and behaves with absolute dominion, the very foundations of culture begin to crumble' (117).

When this happens, 'man sets himself up in the place of God and ends up provoking a rebellion on the part of nature' (117).

The encyclical explicitly acknowledges that an inadequate presentation of Christian anthropology has given rise to a wrong understanding of the relationship between human beings and the world (116). The Human, therefore, needs to be decentred in order to be reconnected within a larger scheme of things. Anthropology, therefore, is one of the causes of the ecological crisis, but it is also one of the solutions to this crisis.

How, then, are we to construct an 'adequate anthropology' in the service of ecology; that is, how can we build an anthropology that supports the life and well-being of the whole planet: the plants and animals and humans. Is it possible to develop an anthropology that respects the integrity of creation? This, it seems to me, is one of the challenges that *Laudato Si'* poses for theology in the twenty-first century.

Principles for the Reconstruction of Anthropology for the Twenty-First Century

One of the refrains throughout *Laudato Si'* is that we are all interconnected (16, 42, 240). According to Francis, 'the world, created according to a divine model … is a web of relations' (240). Everything in the world is interconnected (16, 91, 240) and interrelated (91, 92, 120, 137, 141, 142), and interdependent (164).

For Francis, 'it is proper to every living being to tend towards other things, so that throughout the universe we can find any number of constant and secretly interwoven relationships' (240). This view stands out in stark contrast to the individualism, autonomy and self-sufficiency of modernity. The encyclical goes on to point out that:

> **The person grows more, matures more and is sanctified more to the extent that he or she enters into relationships, going out from themselves to live in communion with God, with others and with all creatures. (240)**

Here Francis is doing two things. First of all, he is pointing us towards a kenotic, self-emptying anthropology based on the Paschal Mystery of Christ as mentioned in Vatican II in *Gaudium et Spes*.[5] Secondly, he is seeking to retrieve the vision of the pre-modern era that assumed an integrated and seamless relationship between God, the self and the cosmos. How, then, are we to understand the human in the twenty-first century? What shape do we give to the human? What might the ingredients of a new anthropology look like? To begin to answer these questions I want to suggest that the shape of the Human is Relational, Dialogical, Embodied, Linguistic, and no longer at the centre of the universe.

The Ingredients of a Chastened Anthropology

In the first instance, pride of place must be given to the primacy of relationality in any reconstruction of what it means to be human in the twenty-first century. This means, in effect, going beyond the enduring influence of Rene Descartes (1596–1650) and his dictum: 'I think, therefore, I am'. This outlook must be replaced by an anthropology that recognises first of all that 'we are, before I am', or, as an African proverb puts it 'we relate, therefore I am'.

Reflecting on evolution, Teilhard de Chardin said, 'What comes first in the world for our thought is not "being" but "union" which produces this being.'[6] For Teilhard, being is first a 'we' before it can become an 'I'.[7] Relationality precedes the historical emergence of individuality. To exist, therefore, is always to coexist, to be is to be in relation, being (*esse*) is always being towards (*esse ad*). Evidence for this emphasis on the primacy of relationality can be found in the fact that we come into the world in a condition of dependent relationality and in all likelihood will leave the world in a similar state. We do not come into the world with a ready-made self; instead we leave the world with a self, emerging as an unfinished, relational reality, a work-in-progress, or, as Paul's letter to the Ephesians puts it, we are 'God's work of art' (Eph 2:10).

Closely related to this primacy of relationality is the centrality of dialogue in the genesis, development and fulfilment of the self. Dialogue is a theme throughout *Laudato Si'*. It is only in and through dialogue that we come to know who we are. The self is dialogical in origin: we do not arrive in the world with a ready-made self, instead we arrive with a capacity to be a relational self. The self comes to be through dialogical engagement between parents, with parents and with others. Over time the self emerges, historically as a reality that is continually under construction and exists as an ongoing project being shaped continuously by dialogue. It is in the encounter with others that we are constituted as selves and begin to discover who we are.

It is this dialogue with the other that awakens our capacity to be in relationships and to discover, as Vatican II says, that the human is at his or her best in relationship with others, that it is through a process of 'sincere self-giving' that people 'fully discover themselves'.[8] Through ongoing dialogue with the other the identity of the self is shaped. Important links exists between dialogue and the development of human identity.

A third element in the reconstruction of anthropology for the twenty-first century is the importance of recognising that the self exists only as embodied. Human consciousness, human interiority, and human subjectivity are available only as embodied; each of these dimensions of the human is expressed and communicated through the body. The human self is only available through the body and comes alive when the body is touched. The body is the sign, the symbol and the sacrament of the self: to reduce the body to mere matter is to diminish the social self. As the encyclical points out, lack of respect for the human body is closely related to lack of respect for the body of the earth and vice versa. The human is a microcosm, as it were, of the macrocosm of the universe.

In the seventh century, Maximus Confessor (*c*.580–662), who had a sense of the cosmic significance of the Christ-event, pointed out, 'The human person is a laboratory in which everything is concentrated.'[9] Goethe saw the human as the first conversation that nature holds with God.[10] Tom Berry suggests that 'we carry the universe in our being (just) as the universe carries us in its being'.[11] A new and important interdependence is emerging in the relationship between the Human and the universe.

Gerard Manley Hopkins captures this unique relationship between the human and the earth in the following way:

And what is Earth's eye, tongue or heart else, where
Else, but in dear dogged man?[12]

This particular perception of the relationship between the earth and
the human is expressed with similar eloquence by Denise Levertov
in a poem entitled 'Tragic Error':

The earth is the Lord's, we gabbled,
and the fullness thereof –
while we looted and pillaged, claiming indemnity:
...
Surely we were to have been
earth's mind, mirror, reflective source.
Surely our task
was to have been
to love the earth,
to *dress and keep it* like Eden's garden.[13]

A further ingredient in the construction of a viable anthropology
for the twenty-first century is a recognition of the role of language
in the constitution and development of human identity. As human
beings, we inhabit a world of language that is unique to the human
species. We depend on a web of language to discover who we are
and how to communicate with each other. At a popular level,
language is seen as that which describes reality, designed to express
and represent the world as it is.

There is, however, another view of language that suggests that
language is about discovery: opening up an invisible world, of
disclosing the many layers of meaning within the world, and, in
particular, about revealing who, what and where we are within that
world of meaning. Within this latter view, language shapes us and
gives us an identity. In this sense, language is constitutive of human

identity and contributes to the empowerment of human agency. Language resonates within human experience and often has the power to activate creative practices. Language, therefore, is not just an add-on to human nature; instead language is constitutive human identity, representing a multi-layered world of meaning: enabling agency, forming identity, and enlarging freedom.

A further and final ingredient in the reconstruction of anthropology for ecology is the need to go beyond the presence of so much anthropocentrism in our thinking, a challenge highlighted by the new encyclical (68–9, 115–22). We are not the centre of the universe; instead we are part of a much larger story which includes the cosmos, the earth and the human community. As the encyclical states, 'We are part of nature, included in it and thus in constant interaction with it' (139).

We need to overcome the gap between the natural world and the human world that has been allowed to develop since the enlightenment. It is this gap, as the encyclical notes, that is one of the root causes of the ecological crisis. Due to this gap, the human has developed an exaggerated sense of his/her own importance and assumed a licence to exploit the earth. The current ecological crisis is not only a moral issue, it is also a deeply anthropological and theological issue. As far back as 1967, the scientists Lynn White could write that 'in its western form, Christianity is the most anthropocentric religion the world has seen'.[14]

Vatican II began to move beyond this anthropocentrism, with some – limited – success.[15] *Laudato Si'* mandates a renewed anthropology in the service of ecology.

This means recognising that the human exists in a unique, relational, embodied, dialogical, linguistic relationship with the rest of creation. Further, it requires that we see the human as part of a long cosmic story. This belongingness of the human within this larger perspective is often expressed poetically by scientists in the following way: the human is cosmic dust in a state of consciousness, freedom and responsibility; the universe shivers with wonder in the depth of the human;[16] we are all made of the ashes of dead stars;[17] we are star-stuff and earth-dust.[18] On the basis of this reconstruction of the human we can now move on to part three.

The Theological Foundations of *Laudato Si'*

One of the underlying themes in the encyclical is, as we have seen, the vision that everything in the world is interconnected, interrelated and interdependent. This vision underpins the entire encyclical. According to Francis, the accounts of creation in Genesis:

> **suggest human life is grounded in three fundamental and closely intertwined relations: with God, with our neighbour and with the earth. (66)**

It is important to note here the importance given to our relationship with the earth. The encyclical challenges us to keep these three realities together and Francis does this by talking about the action of the Spirit of God in the world and the centrality of Christ to the whole of creation.

The Unifying Action of the Spirit in the World: Pneumatology

There is a Spirit-driven theology animating much of the vision of Pope Francis, both in this encyclical and in his other writings.[19] If you want to understand what it is that fires the vision of Francis, watch out for his references to the gift of the Spirit. Let us draw together some of the scattered references to the Holy Spirit in *Laudato Si'*. The encyclical points out:

The Spirit of God has filled the universe with possibilities and therefore, from the very heart of things, something new can always emerge. (80)

Note that it says the Holy Spirit fills the universe. We are more accustomed to talking about the Spirit in the life of the individual and the life of the Church, but not so much in the universe. This emphasis retrieves the biblical awareness of the Spirit of God suffusing the whole of creation (Gn 1:1–2:25, Ps 104:29 and 139:7–15; Job 34:14–15; Ez 39:5–15). Secondly, it says something new can always emerge out of this universe filled with the Holy Spirit. Francis sees the Spirit as the source of creativity in our world. In support of what he is saying, he quotes John Paul II as follows:

The Holy Spirit can be said to possess an infinite creativity, proper to the divine mind, which knows how to loosen the knots of human affairs, including the most complex and inscrutable. (80)

Many have seen the Spirit primarily as the principle of stability and supporter of the status quo, protecting the Church through trials and tribulations. In contrast, Francis is suggesting that the Spirit is the source of creativity in the world and in the Church. This perception of the Spirit is repeated again towards the end of the encyclical:

The Spirit … is intimately present at the very heart of the universe, inspiring and bringing new pathways. (238)

The Spirit, therefore, is the source of creativity and the animating power behind what is new and emergent in our world. This vision of the Spirit as present in the universe and as the source of creativity is grounded in the Bible as we shall see presently.

Many associate the Revelation of the Spirit in the Bible with the outpouring of the Spirit at Pentecost. One of the problems, however, with this particular perception of the Spirit is that it short-changes the action of the Spirit in creation, in the history of Israel, and in the life of Jesus as if they were somehow Spirit-less. Instead we must go back further before the life of Jesus, before the history of Israel, to the dawn of time and beginning of creation to discover the presence of the Spirit in the world.

Reading the first story of creation in the Book of Genesis, we see the Spirit of God is actively involved at the very beginning of Creation: 'In the beginning when God created the heavens and the earth, the earth was a formless void ... a wind from God swept over the face of the earth' (Gn 1:1–2).

There are a number of points worth noting about these opening verses of the Bible. First of all, the breath of God, the Spirit of God, is involved at the very beginning, at the dawn of time. Secondly, we are told that the Spirit of God 'swept over the face of the earth'. A better translation would be that the Spirit of God was brooding over the earth, or hatching over the earth, or warming the earth like the mother hen in a nest.

A third point is that it is this presence of the Spirit at the dawn of time that facilitates the utterance of the Word of God, 'Let there be light', just as the human breath enables the uttering of human words. Thus, the presence of the Spirit precedes the action of the Word of God. This creative action of the Spirit of God is even more explicit in the second story of creation, which is about the creation of man and woman (Gn 2:4–25). There we read: 'God formed the human from the dust of the ground and breathed into his nostril the breath of life; and the human became a living being' (Gn 2:7).

Again, a few points of commentary may be helpful here. First of all, it is the breath of God that gives rise to life and it is the same breath present at the beginning, brooding over the earth, that is now active in the creation of human beings. Secondly, the human is formed out of the earth, out of the dust of the ground, and, therefore, the human might more properly be called 'an earthling' or 'a worldling' or 'a groundling'. The Hebrew word for the earth is *adamah*, and the Hebrew word for the human is *adam*; thus, there is a link between the earth and the human that is lost in translation. The third point worth noting is that there is an intimate link, from the beginning, between the Spirit and creation, as well as between the Spirit and human beings. Creation, the whole of creation, from the beginning, is Spirit-endowed. The whole of creation, the whole of nature, all creatures and all human beings, are the dwelling places of the Spirit of God in varying degrees, or, as one commentator puts it, the whole of creation is 'en-spirited by God' from the very beginning.[20] This theology of the Spirit in the stories of creation is continued in the other books of the Hebrew scriptures such as the Psalms 104:29, 139:7–15; Ezekiel 37:5–15; Job 34:14–15, 33:4.

In the New Testament, there are many references to the action of the Spirit: in the life of Mary, especially at the Annunciation; throughout the life of Jesus; and in the new messianic communities. Suffice to say that the life of Jesus from the beginning to end is Spirit-driven, culminating in the Pentecostal event which is not just the outpouring of the Spirit of God, but the outpouring of the distinctive Spirit of Christ. A number of scripture scholars describe Pentecost as 'the Big Bang moment of Christianity'.[21]

Most theologians agree that this biblical emphasis on the Spirit requires that we in the West overcome the dualism that has been allowed to develop between Spirit and matter, body and soul, the Sacred and the earth. All emphasise that the Spirit is only available and active as embodied in creation, guiding Israel, personalised in

Christ, and indwelling the early messianic community of Christians. The action of the Spirit does not bypass the materiality of the world in which we live.

One of the twentieth century Catholic thinkers to address this dualism within the modern era was Teilhard de Chardin (1881–1955). Teilhard as a scientist sought to bring Christianity into dialogue with evolution. He had much to say about Christ. He also had a few striking statements about the Spirit which are worth noting. For example, in an essay, written in 1919, entitled 'The Spiritual Power of Matter', he composed a 'Hymn to Matter'. In that well-known hymn, he chants:

> Blessed be you, harsh matter
> Blessed be you, perilous matter
> Blessed be you, mighty matter
> I acclaim you (that is matter)
> As the divine milieu,
> charged with creative power
> as the ocean stirred by the Spirit
> as the clay moulded and infused
> by the incarnate Word.[22]

Throughout his life, Teilhard was fascinated by matter, by the life and energy and dynamism of matter as a scientist, but also as a Christian, because he saw the creative Spirit of God as continuously active in matter. Later, in 1936, he returned to this theme:

> All that exists is matter becoming Spirit. There is neither Spirit nor matter in the world; the stuff of the universe is spirit-matter. No other substance but this could produce the human molecule.[23]

Many may have had difficulty accepting the theory of evolution until they read Teilhard. Their question was: How can you move from inert matter to life? Teilhard says: There is no such thing as pure matter; all of matter is infused with Spirit and destined for spiritual realisation in the emergence of the human. Teilhard's vision resonates with the Spirit-centred stories of creation in the books of the Hebrew scriptures.

It is this sense of creation as Spirit-endowed that Pope Francis is trying to recover in the service on an integral ecology. Unless and until we rediscover the existence of *life within the earth*, of *Spirit within* matter, and of the *sacred within* the secular, there will be little ecological change and even less ecological conversion. Others, such as Karl Rahner, Henri de Lubac, Tom Berry, Denis Edwards, Ilia Delio and Elizabeth A. Johnson, have stood on the shoulders Teilhard's vision.

The Centrality of Christ: Christology

The second theological foundation supporting the encyclical is, as you would expect, the person of Christ. Again like the Spirit, references to Christ are scattered throughout the encyclical. There is no attempt to present a systematic Christology; however, there are enough pointers to indicate the kind of Christology informing the encyclical. There are a few brief references to the historical Jesus living a life 'in touch with nature' (97, 98). The encyclical notes that Jesus employs images from nature to communicate his teaching about the Reign of God. And then the encyclical makes a number of Christological statements worth noting. In general the encyclical notes that 'the destiny of creation is bound up with the mystery of Christ' (99).

This linking of Christ with creation is unpacked with specific reference to the Resurrection and Incarnation. In relation to the Resurrection, the encyclical points out:

The ultimate destiny of the universe is in the fullness of God, and this has already been obtained by the risen Christ, the measure of the maturity of all things. (83)

Elsewhere it says:

Christ has taken unto himself this material world and now, risen, is intimately present to each being, surrounding it with his affection and penetrating it with his light. (221, 100)

This vision is repeated once again towards the end of the encyclical in the striking statement that 'Creation has reached the fullness of its beauty in the risen Christ' (241). A further reference to the Resurrection is that the risen humanity of Christ is 'the pledge of the final transfiguration of all created reality' (237).

In the first three references above the emphasis is on the bodily Resurrection of Christ from the dead and embrace what some theologians call 'Deep Resurrection'; that is a recognition that the Resurrection reaches deep down into the materiality of the world. Not only does the Resurrection affect the very core of humanity but it also touches the centre of creation.

In the fourth reference to Resurrection it is claimed that the reality of the risen Christ is the pledge of the final transfiguration of all reality. In other words, Deep Resurrection, or 'cosmic resurrection', assures us that humanity and creation have a future together and that this future has been pre-fingered embryonically in the bodily resurrection of Christ. The Resurrection of Christ is an anticipation of the end, a disclosure of the future, a preview of the life to come, the culmination of the process of evolution, and a prototype of the end of time.[24] This cosmic outreach of the Resurrection of Christ is intimated in the Pauline letters, which present Christ as 'the first born of all creation' (Col 1:15) and a 'New Creation' (2 Cor 5:17; Gal 6:15).

In a similar vein, Ambrose of Milan (340–97) proclaimed that 'In Christ's Resurrection, the earth itself arose' and the Exultet hymn of the liturgy for the Easter vigil, declares, 'Exult all creation, around God's throne ... Rejoice, O Earth, in shining splendour, radiant in the brightness of your King.'[25] In brief, Christ, the risen Christ, is the crown of creation, or as Teilhard would put it Christ is the Omega point in the evolution of the universe.[26]

Alongside the Resurrection, there is also an emphasis on the importance of the Incarnation: 'through the Incarnation, the mystery of Christ is at work in a hidden way in the natural world' (99). Further, it is pointed out that 'the Son of God has incorporated in his person part of the material world, planting in it a seed of definitive transformation' (235). And later it is noted that Christ 'has united himself definitively to our earth' (245).

In these three scattered references we see an equally important play on the Incarnation as reaching deep down into the materiality of creation. The doctrine of the Incarnation is about the eternal Word of God becoming flesh in Jesus: the Word became not only human (*anthropos*) but also flesh (*sarx*) which is cosmic dust enlivened by the breath of God. This emphasis on flesh (*sarx*) connects the Word of God not only to the whole of humanity made up of flesh but also to the ancient cosmic dust that evolved into flesh through the breath of God.

The Word of God, enfleshed in Jesus, is, therefore, linked to the whole of humanity and the wider community of life on earth that has its origins in the evolution of the cosmos. If we can appreciate the human as cosmic dust in a state of consciousness and, therefore, every human being as a child of the cosmos, including Jesus, then we should be able to appreciate the Word (the *Logos*) wedded to the human, to the flesh of the earth and the dust of cosmos. The Incarnation reaches into the core of humanity and the heart of the creation.[27]

In these few scattered references Francis is holding up the Resurrection and the Incarnation as the basis of an ecological Christology; he is seeking to recover the forgotten cosmic dimensions of both Resurrection and Incarnation; he is expanding the Christological imagination to embrace the earth.

What is really significant about these statements is a footnote attached to paragraph eighty-three which refers us to 'the contribution of Fr Teilhard de Chardin'. By giving a footnote to Teilhard de Chardin, Francis is not only rehabilitating him, but pointing us in a particular direction, namely the need for a new Christology, a Cosmic Christology of the type put forward by Teilhard, a Christology that is able to take account of evolution and has the capacity to locate Christ at the centre of creation.

From the late 1950s through to the 1990s the quest for the historical Jesus was at the centre of a lot of Christology. Now, in the light of the ecological crisis and, in particular, *Laudato Si'*, the quest for the historical Jesus needs to be complemented by an equally important quest for the cosmic Christ. Traces of the presence of the cosmic Christ can be found in the creation-centred Christologies of the New Testament.

The Creation-Centred Christologies of the New Testament

It should be noted that the earliest Christologies in Paul are creation-centred, especially the Christologies of Colossians (Col 1:15–29), Ephesians (Eph 1:7–10), Philippians (Phil 2:10–11), first and second Corinthians (1 Cor 15:20–8, 2 Cor 5:9). Further, the confession of Jesus as the Wisdom of God in first Corinthians (1 Cor 1:24, 30) is also a creation-centred Christology, given the role of wisdom within creation in the Hebrew scriptures (Prov 8:22–31). In addition, there is a creation-centred Christology in the complex Adam-Christ typology of Romans 5:18–21.[28] The reference to Adam in Romans 5 is a way highlighting the universal and cosmic significance of the Christ-event. Of course, the fullest statement of a cosmic Christology in the New Testament is to be found in the John's prologue:

In the beginning was the Word, the Word was with God …
And the Word was made flesh and dwelt among us. (Jn 1:1, 14)

For Paul and John, there is a deep theological awareness of the cosmic outreach and significance of the Christ-event. Within the early New Testament creation-centred Christologies, we see a close link between Creation and Incarnation. Creation is the basis of Incarnation and Incarnation is the fulfilment of creation.[29] Put in contemporary terms, we might see Christology as 'concentrated creation': what happens in Christology is a crystallisation of the ongoing drama taking place in creation.[30]

What these creation-centred Christologies imply is that humanity history and creation have a future and an ultimate destiny. In the light of these Christologies we can say: that the unfolding of creation and the evolution of humanity are not rudderless; that each one of us is not just a spark in the evolutionary spiral that one day will burn out; that humans are not just shooting stars destined to disappear into empty space of dark matter.

Instead as the US theologian Zachary Hayes says, echoing Teilhard, Tom Berry and Rahner, 'a cosmos without Christ is a cosmos without a head … But with Christ, all the lines of energy are coordinated and unified … all is finally brought to its destiny in God.'[31]

To sum up and to conclude, I am suggesting that the seeds of a new anthropology are present in *Laudato Si'*, and that the theological foundations of an integral ecology are outlined in embryo in *Laudato Si'* in terms of a cosmic pneumatology and cosmic Christologies.

Endnotes

1. John Paul II, 'Message to the Reverend George Coyne SJ, Director of the Vatican Observatory', in Robert Russell, William Stoeger and George Coyne (eds), *Physics, Philosophy and Theology: A Common Quest for Understanding*, Vatican City: Vatican Observatory, 1988, M13.

2. John Paul II, *Message to the Pontifical Academy of Sciences: On Evolution*, 22 October 1996.

3. Stephen Hawking, *A Brief History of Time*, New York: Bantam Books, 1988, pp. 121–2.

4. I am using the word 'man' in a non-inclusive sense in this particular instance.

5. *Gaudium et Spes*, 24.

6. P. Teilhard de Chardin, *Christianity and Evolution: Reflections on Science and Religion*, Orlando: Harcourt, 1971, p. 227.

7. See Ilia Delio, 'Evolution and the rise of the secular God', *From Teilhard to Omega: Co-creating an Unfinished Universe*, New York: Orbis Books, 2014, pp. 42–3.

8. *Gaudium et Spes*, 24.

9. See Ambiguum 41, in *On the Cosmic Mystery of Jesus Christ: Selected Writings from St Maximus the Confessor*, New York: St Vladimir's Seminary Press, 2004, p. 157.

10. Taken from Gabriel Daly, *Creation and Redemption*, Dublin: Gill and Macmillan, 1988, 116.

11. Tom Berry, *The Dream of the Earth*, San Francisco: Sierra Club Books, 1988, p. 132.

12. G.M. Hopkins, 'Ribblesdale', 1918.

13. Denise Levertov, 'Tragic Error', 1993.

14. Lynn White, 'The Historical Roots of Our Ecological Crisis', *Science*, 155:3767, 1967, p. 1205.

15. This point is developed further in Dermot A. Lane, *Catholic Education in the Light of Vatican II and Laudato Si'*, Dublin: Veritas, 2015, pp. 38–44.

16. Brian Swimme, *The Universe is a Green Dragon: The Cosmic Creation Story*, New Mexico: Bear and Company, 1984, p. 32.

17. John Polkinghorne, *One World: The Interaction of Science and Theology*, London: SPCK, 1986, p. 56.

18. Elizabeth A. Johnson, *Ask the Beasts: Darwin and the God of love*, New York: Bloomsbury, 2014, p. 109.

19. For example, his apostolic exhortation, *The Joy of the Gospel*, is peppered with references to the spirit. One word count suggests 175 references to the Spirit, with 253 to Christ. Such word counts, of course, are of limited doctrinal significance. It is worth noting that on the day of the beatification of John XXIII and John Paul II what Francis praised most was their openness and receptivity to the action of the Spirit. In his homily opening the 2014 extraordinary synod of bishops he warned: 'We can thwart God's dream if we fail to let ourselves be guided by the Holy Spirit.' This is an echo of what Karl Rahner wrote on the eve of the Second Vatican Council.

20. Jay McDaniel, '"Where is the Holy Spirit Anyway?" Response to a Sceptic Environmentalist', *Ecumenical Review*, 42:2, 1990, pp. 162–74.

21. James Dunne, *Beginning from Jerusalem* (*Christianity in the Making*, vol. 2), Michigan: Eerdmans, 2009, p. 162; Amos Yong, *Who Is the Holy Spirit: A Walk with the Apostles?*, MA: Paraclete Press, 2011 p. 12.

22. P. Teilhard de Chardin, *Hymn of the Universe*, London: Collins, 1965, p. 68–70.

23. P. Teilhard de Chardin, *Human Energy*, London: Collins, 1969, p. 57–8.

24. See Dermot A. Lane, *Keeping Hope Alive: Stirrings in Christian Theology*, New York: Paulist Press, 1996/2005, p. 125.

25. These cosmic perspectives on Christology are developed more extensively in Dermot A. Lane, 'Whither the World', *Keeping Hope Alive*, pp. 174–93, especially pp. 187–93, and explicitly in Johnson, *Ask the Beasts*, pp. 207–10.

26. P. Teilhard de Chardin, *Christianity and Evolution*, p. 77.

27. On the cosmic significance of the Incarnation see Dermot A. Lane, 'The Doctrine of the Incarnation: Human and Cosmic Considerations', *Christ at the Centre: Selected Issues in Christology*, New York: Paulist Press, 1990, pp. 130–58, and Johnson, *Ask the Beasts*, pp. 192–9.

28. This Adam Christology of Paul is also present, though less obviously, in 1 Cor 15:21–2 and Phil 2:6–11.

29. Dermot A. Lane, *The Reality of Jesus: An Essay in Christology*, Dublin: Veritas/New York: Paulist Press, 1975/2000, pp. 134–45.

30. Edward Schillebeeckx, *Interim Report on the Books of Jesus Christ*, New York: Crossroad, 1982, p. 128.

31. Z. Hayes, 'Christ, Word of God and Exemplar of Humanity', *Cord*, 46:1, 1996, p. 13.

Creation as Incarnation: Reflections on Biodiversity in *Laudato Si'*

JOHN FEEHAN

In the fabulous compendium of Irish Early Christian lore and practice known as the *Martyrology of Óengus* there is an anecdote about the mysterious St Molua, who lived in the second half of the sixth century. It recalls an occasion when, while out for a walk, St Mael Anfaidh encountered a small bird wailing and sorrowing by the side of the road. As he wondered what this could mean, an angel informed him, 'Mo Lua, son of Ocha, has died, and that is why the living things bewail him, for he never killed a living thing, great nor small; not more do men bewail him than the other living things do, and among them the little bird that you see.'[1]

Ciarán of Saighir lived as a hermit in fifth-century Ireland, where, in the wilderness of south-west Offaly, his first monks were fox and badger, deer and wild boar. And, of course, similar tales of kinship exist about Francis of Assisi, who spoke of Friar Wolf and made nests for his little sisters, the wild turtle doves. From the life of Ciarán of Saighir, there is a wonderful tale:

When St Ciarán arrived at Saighir, the first thing he did was sit under a certain tree, in whose shade a ferocious wild boar was lying. At first when he saw the man, the boar fled in terror, but then he was made gentle by God, and he came back to Ciarán as if he had known him all his life: and that boar became a disciple of Ciarán in that place just like any monk. And he assiduously rooted up bushes and hay with which the holy man could make his cell. At this time, no man lived with Ciarán, because he had escaped from his disciples to his remote place on his own. But afterwards other animals came out of their lairs in the wilderness to St Ciarán: namely a fox, a badger, and a wolf and a deer: they remained tame in his presence, and obeyed him in everything, just as though they were monks.

But the day came when the fox, being shiftier and more sly than the other animals, stole the sandals of his abbot, holy Ciarán himself, and, abandoning his vocation, took them away with him to his former lair in the wilderness, wishing to eat them there in peace. Knowing this, holy father Ciarán called another of his monks to him, namely the badger, and sent him into the wilderness after the fox, so that he might bring back his erring brother. The badger, because he was a creature skilled in the ways of the woods, obediently headed off in search of the thief, quickly picked up the trail and arrived at the lair of Brother Fox. Finding him about to eat his lord's sandals, the badger cut off the fox's two ears and his tail, and beat him up, and then compelled him to come back with him to his monastery, so that he might atone for his theft. The fox, having little choice in the matter, accompanied the badger, and they arrived back with the sandals undamaged. And the holy man said to the fox, 'Brother, why have you done this evil thing which does not become a monk. You know that the water here is sweet and free to us all, and likewise we all eat the same food?

And if you had a yearning for flesh, almighty God would have provided it from the trees of the wood for us to give to you.' So then the fox, begging forgiveness, did penance for his deed, and from then on he only ate what he was told to eat, living out his days as one of the brothers.[2]

In the vast and colourful tapestry that is the history of Christianity we find here and there these flecks of green thread that represent occasional intimations of kinship and compassion between ourselves and animals, but these threads contribute nothing to the great pageant of creation, salvation and redemption depicted there. The tapestry is abundantly adorned with plant and animal life, but only as the backdrop to the great drama that is being enacted centre stage, in which the actors are human beings, made in the image of God. These others were created in the first instance to be at the service of mankind, 'the most perfect of the animals, since in the order of perfection it ranks highest', as St Albert describes us: a view of the relationship rooted in the traditional and mistaken understanding of the infamous verses in Genesis 1 in which God confers mastery upon us:

Let us make man in our image, after our likeness: and let them have dominion over the fish of the sea, and over the fowl of the air, and over the cattle, and over every creeping thing that creepeth upon the earth.[3]

This view of the relationship between God, ourselves and other forms of life is copper-fastened in traditional mainstream theology. 'Reason has not been given to [animals] to have in common with us', wrote St Augustine, 'and so, by the most just ordinances of the Creator, both their life and their death is subject to our use.' In the opinion of Thomas Aquinas: 'It is not wrong for man to make use of [animals] either by killing them or in any other way whatever.'[4] In more modern vein, the Jesuit theologian Joseph Rickaby – echoing the traditional view of what creation is for held as firmly by Martin Luther and John Calvin as by Thomas Aquinas – wrote: 'Brute beasts, not having understanding and therefore not being persons, cannot have any rights ... We have no duties of charity, nor duties of any kind to the lower animals, as neither to sticks and stones.'[5] And as recently as 1994 the Catholic Catechism stated that 'God willed creation as a gift addressed to man ... Animals, like plants and inanimate beings, are by nature destined for the common good of past, present and future humanity.'[6]

Down the centuries this understanding of the relationship between God and his creatures has been graphically represented by images of the Great Chain of Being, which ranked other creatures below us at intervals that reflected their similarity to us humans, just as it ranked angels and saints at intervals above, between ourselves and God in his heaven.

But just as the progress of scientific understanding of how creation actually works has transformed the way we see the cosmos and our human understanding of the fabric of reality, so too, and indeed as part of that broader expansion of the human horizon on cosmic reality in its quest for God, has it transformed our biological appreciation of what God is about, of how God is at work in the world.

Central to this advance was the technological progress that made the microscope possible, and which began to give us new eyes: eyes that can see what has always been before us, but hidden. We were the first privileged enough to see what (as Thomas Browne put it) had been hidden from all the ages before us. Central also was the technological advance that enabled us to visit the deepest recesses of the oceans, the outermost horizons where life is possible.

The two axes around which our biological understanding has been utterly revolutionised can be described under the headings of complexity and affinity. Everything that lives is comparably complex biologically. The cells of other creatures, the building blocks of the body, are no less complex than our human cells. But just stating it like that gives no sense of how mesmerisingly complex every living creature, plant no less than animal, is. But to be truly overwhelmed by this requires knowledge of biology; the deeper that knowledge the greater the depth to which you are overwhelmed.

The Diversity of Life on Earth

Our modern understanding of the theological significance of life on earth begins with the work of the great English naturalist John Ray (1627–1705), who is best remembered today for his monumental contribution to the description and cataloguing of the diversity and complexity of plant and animal life at a time when the scale of diversity and the nature of complexity (and particularly the ways in which plants and animals are adapted for their particular ways of life) were beginning to be appreciated. For him what this demonstrated was the greatness of the God who was behind it: the 'Wisdom of God' as he calls it in the title of his seminal summary of his reflections in this area.[7]

We must not forget the profound antithesis between the natural and the supernatural, the material and the spiritual, that had led Christianity between the third and the sixteenth centuries – in both Catholic and Protestant spirituality and theology – to a scorn and depreciation of nature. John Ray's open delight in the beauty, order and complexity of the natural world – on a sensory, aesthetic level first of all, augmented by growing understanding and appreciation on an intellectual level, and constantly alert to its spiritual significance – is 'in striking contrast to the philosophy and religion both of the Catholic and the Protestant traditions'.

> To Augustine as to Luther nature belonged to a plane irrelevant if not actually hostile to religion. Its beauty was a temptation, its study a waste of time, its meaning so distorted that there is a radical difference between nature and grace ... But the direct insistence upon the essential unity of natural and revealed, as alike proceeding from and integrated by the divine purpose, had not found clear and well-informed expression until Ray's book was published.[8]

Ray's *The Wisdom of God Manifested in the Works of Creation* was profoundly influential (going through four editions in his lifetime, and many more after), most immediately perhaps through its influence on William Paley's *Natural Theology*, to which Charles Darwin acknowledged his indebtedness.[9] In the preface to the definitive edition of his book, published in 1826 (and so just before organic evolution moved to centre stage in biology, just before our human capacity to focus on that fourth dimension of time began to come properly into focus) Ray attempted 'to run over all the visible works of God in particular, and to trace the footsteps of his wisdom in the composition, order, harmony, and uses of every one of them, as well as of those that I have selected'. But to do so, he wrote, would be a task not only 'far transcending my skill and abilities; nay, the joint skill and endeavours of all men now living, or that shall live after a thousand ages, should the world last so long.'[10]

In John Ray's day, the number of species – in his words 'known to science, as the saying goes' – was under forty thousand.[11] But while he acknowledged that this was an underestimate – 'How many of each genus remain yet undiscovered, one cannot certainly nor very nearly conjecture; but we may suppose the whole sum of beasts and birds to exceed by a third part, and fishes by one half, those known.'[12] – he can have had no idea whatever of the extent of that underestimate.

To date something like 1.7 million species have been described. Half of these are insects, some two hundred and fifty thousand are vascular plants and bryophytes, forty-one thousand are vertebrates; and then the rest. But this is only the number of those that have been formally described. The true number of multicellular species is likely to be between ten and thirty million. Whether the figure is five or thirty million scarcely matters as far as our human ability to get our head around such numbers is concerned: to comprehend even a million is beyond us.

Astronomical sums of time are so great that they bankrupt the imagination. We listen to the geologists and physicists wrangling over their accounts and compounding vast historical debts with the relish of usurers, but it is all one to us after the first million years.[13]

As we struggle to identify order within this bewildering diversity, there is a danger implicit in taxonomy that we think of them in terms somewhat analogous to a vast, colourful stamp collection to be sorted. And here, perhaps, we face the greatest challenge. For every one of these millions is biologically as complex as I am, made with the same loving care, unfolded from the same seed of being at the beginning of things, has travelled an evolutionary journey similar to mine, from the same starting point, but in a different and complementary direction.

Actual numbers of species are only one aspect, one measure, of the diversity of life. The other is diversity at the level of groups or organisms. To get a sense of this, consider two of the most popular university textbooks on biodiversity: Barnes' *The Diversity of Life on Earth*[14] and *Five Kingdoms* by Lynn Margulis and Karlene Schwartz.[15] These are a sort of who's who of life, a taxonomic equivalent of our human biographical dictionaries, in which each group is allocated space proportional to its biological stature, just as in these dictionaries the number of words is (supposedly) proportional to the significance of the individual in question.

In Barnes' book, insects – which as we have just seen account for half the living species that have been described – occupy a mere five or six pages out of the total of three hundred and forty five. The rest is taken up with the remaining eighty-eight phyla of life on earth; each as deserving of its few pages as the next. Vertebrates – mammals, birds, reptiles, amphibians and fishes – get eight pages. Mammals get half a page. In the three hundred or so descriptive pages of Margulis and Swartz (third edition), vertebrates and their relatives merit a mere five out of a total of five hundred and twenty pages. The rest is given over to similarly concise descriptive accounts of all the other groups of equally complex organisms. A few of these are familiar to be sure – molluscs, crustaceans, annelids – but most are likely to be unfamiliar, even to many biologists: Gnathostomulids, Rhombozoa, Orthonectida, Nematomorphs, Acanthocephala, Kinorynchs, Priapulida, Gastrotrichs, Loricifera, Entoprocts, Pogonophora and Onychophora to name at random a dozen of the thirty-seven phyla of animals listed in Margulis and Schwartz.

Insects are divided into thirty-four groups known as 'orders'. The common names of some are familiar, such as butterflies, beetles, dragonflies, while others are less so. But we know little about the lives of the overwhelming majority, even of those that have been formally described and named – never mind those that have not, and in all likelihood never well be. Yet each represents a unique and marvellous achievement of living possibility. It is difficult to convey in words any real impression of the ingenuity with which every possible mode of existence is exploited through this kaleidoscopic natural diversity. Every possible source of energy and material is utilised – and most of this is hidden from us. The more deeply you can immerse yourself in these wonderful creatures, the more you come to understand their complexity and their beauty, the adaptations each of them has developed on its unique evolutionary journey, which fit each of them to its unique mode of living, the closer you appreciate them as the Divine Mind appreciates them.

No more than we can relate visually to particle physics can we relate fully to this, but to the extent we can, we touch the hem of God's own self-fulfilment in being.

Biodiversity and *Laudato Si'*

An appreciation of all of this is the essential foundation for the remarkable passages in *Laudato Si'* on the meaning and worth of individual species. It is precisely its rootedness in this essential biological foundation that gives these passages their unprecedented colour and depth. It is only against this background that we can properly appreciate the conversion to which the encyclical calls us in this regard:

> The creatures of the earth were not created in the first instance for us to dispose of as we will, regardless of their place in God's plan. They are primarily for 'the fulfilment of God's own unfolding plan for Creation.' (53)

> Together with our obligation to use the earth's goods responsibly, we are called to recognise that other living beings have a value of their own in God's eyes: 'by their mere existence they bless him and give him glory' (*CCC*, 2416). (69)

> Each of the various creatures, willed in its own being, reflects in its own way a ray of God's infinite wisdom and goodness. Man must therefore respect the particular goodness of every

creature, to avoid any disordered use of things. (69)
Creation is 'God's loving plan in which every creature has its own value and significance.' (76)

Even the fleeting lives of the least of beings is the object of his love, and in its few seconds of existence, God enfolds it with his affection. (77)

Each creature has its own purpose. (84)

Everything is, as it were, a caress of God. (84)[16]

Our meditation upon the meaning of it all is deepened as the progress of understanding of the nature of creation's diversity makes it ever clearer to us that creation is not in the first instance for us. 'Each creature has its own purpose,' *Laudato Si'* reminds us (84). 'The ultimate purpose of other creatures is not to be found in us. Rather, all creatures are moving forward with us and through us to a common point of arrival, which is God' (83). Only such meditation will bring home to us the depth of truth in which such phrases in the encyclical are rooted.

This meditation begins with attention. Pope Francis speaks of the 'mystical meaning to be found' in the smallest detail. The example he chooses is a leaf (233).[17] He quotes Patriarch Bartholomew, 'It is our humble conviction that the divine and the humble meet in the slightest detail in the seamless garment of God's creation, in the last speck of dust in our planet' (9). The passage continues:

The ideal is not only to pass from the exterior to the interior to discover the action of God in the soul, but also to discover God in all things. Saint Bonaventure teaches us that 'contemplation deepens the more we feel the working of God's grace within our

hearts, and the better we learn to encounter God in creatures outside ourselves.' (233)

Read this again carefully. Traditionally we might perhaps have registered the first part of this sentence with greater force: 'contemplation deepens the more we feel the working of God's grace within our hearts'; but now we need to register the second part with equal appreciation: 'contemplation deepens the better we learn to encounter God in creatures outside ourselves.'

But this calls on us to stop where we are and to look, and in the engagement that follows, sensory, rational and conative, to attend. When Jesus says, 'Consider the lilies ...' he is saying, in so many words if we think deeply enough about it, drop everything for a time and come, follow in this direction, along this other dimension that takes us through and beyond time. The injunction to consider the lilies can be a little misleading since for us 'lilies' are exotic, flamboyant flowers in gardens and florists, fit for the altar. But in the Middle East they are the weeds of the wayside, the Palestinian equivalent of dandelions and daisies and primroses on the edge of our cultivated fields.

Evolution in *Laudato Si'*

A profoundly important aspect of biodiversity that can easily escape our first reading of the encyclical – and indeed our second or hundredth reading of it – is that this wondrous 'web of life', this rainbow of living diversity, cannot be described in the three dimensions of space. Indeed, to confine it to these dimensions of the present – and although as such it defies beyond measure our human capacity to take it all in – is to miss something absolutely central to its ultimate meaning.

The biodiversity of our age is but a still frame in a moving narrative. We now see that the mesmerising abundance of life on earth is not defined by the tiny fraction of it that we humans experience or can experience: the still frame in this moving narrative which is all that we can experience, our time on earth confined as it is to the last hundred thousand years. Although it is possible to argue that living diversity had reached a peak around the time humans first appeared on earth, there has been comparable diversity during every period of geological time, always different, the mesmerising biodiversity of any one period of geological time – which few but palaeontologists are privileged to wonder at – an efflorescence of hitherto unexpressed embryonic possibility.[18]

The touch of *Laudato Si'* on this fundamental fourth dimension and its implications is gentle: God's divine presence '*continues* the work of creation' (80); 'The universe *unfolds* in God, who fills it completely' (233); 'Faith allows us to interpret the meaning and the mysterious beauty of what is *unfolding*' (79). This is done with the gentle touch of a feather. Despite its explosive spiritual significance, this is explored no further. The reason for this is most likely ecclesiastical diplomacy, guaranteed as it is in this age of our theological infancy to stir up a hornets' nest of conservative outrage in the Church, particularly in those quarters where Pope Francis is trying to wrestle with conservative opinion in other, more immediately pressing issues equally critical to a mature understanding of how God is at work in the world.

The Wonder of Individual Species

It is extraordinarily difficult for us to appreciate the evolutionary achievement individual species represents. We must always start by remembering that this species before me, this flower or woodlouse in the crannied wall, this worm in the soil, stands at the end of an evolutionary journey as long as our human journey; that if we follow the path of that journey backwards through geological time it will meet with ours, because the mesmerisingly complex network of the paths they trace is a family tree. We are all, every species of us, brother and sister to different degrees of consanguinity.[19] The differences that define us are always related to the demands of the different ways of life to which we have become adapted during that long journey.

Each looks out upon, and presents itself to, a world centred on itself, focused through senses that apprehend those elements and dimensions of reality that are relevant to it. Each is, therefore, in essence, a life made possible and supported by a unique combination of the material and energetic resources present in the world. It is the embodiment of these resources, exploiting through them a unique mode of living possibility presented by the evolving cosmos. But when we observe the lives of other creatures we inevitably see them through our own human eyes. We cannot appreciate the fulfilment their being brings, feel as they feel, think as they think, enjoy as they, each in their unique way, enjoy. What, then, can we know of the God they embody and reflect?

Time and again in my growing acquaintance with the lives of particular creatures I have been overwhelmed, mesmerised, by the wonder of their lives. I have meditated on each in turn, sucked into their lives, and every time I have been overwhelmed at the realisation that each is as fully the centre of its world as we are ours. The list of the creatures whose lives I have shared in this intimate way extends to several hundred now, and I never lose sight of the fact that this is the smallest fraction of all there is or was. And how dare I use the word 'intimate' for a mere acquaintance, for it is in truth no more than that. And how must my appreciation pale beside that of the God whose ideas they are, 'intimations of things which for their greater part escape our sensual experience, but which to an increasing consciousness may yield their secrets.'[20]

Saint Albert wrote his magisterial work on the natural history of animals – the first encyclopaedia of biodiversity – during the lifetime of Thomas Aquinas (between 1258 and 1262).[21] In this fantastic book – fantastic in both senses of that word – he gathered together everything that was known about animals in his day. It's full of direct observation, in keeping with his dictum that man's knowledge must begin with an apprehension of reality obtained from direct encounters with nature itself.[22]

The total number of species in Albert's catalogue of all God's creatures ran to just five hundred, overwhelmingly dominated by the ones we could see with our own eyes.[23] And how much more might we expect to know? In one of his sermons, St Columban wrote (c.600 AD) of how little we should expect to know of God's creatures. 'Our small minds are not made for that,' he wrote. 'Think of this world our familiar earth and sea: familiar indeed, and how much we know of them, and how little. What do we know of the teeming life beneath the waves, or even on much of the surface of the earth?'[24] The answer is that today we know an absolutely incredible amount. We know of creatures he could never, ever, have imagined.

There is no more magisterial statement of the theological meaning of biological diversity than that found in St Thomas Aquinas' *Summa Theologiae*:

> God cannot express himself fully in any one creature: and so he has produced many and diverse life forms, so that what one lacks in its expression of divine goodness may be compensated for by others: for goodness, which in God is single and undifferentiated, in creatures is refracted into a myriad hues of being.[25]

But in 1250 our direct encounter with the rest of creation was limited by the fact that it was effectively confined to Europe and the lands just beyond its borders. As for what we knew of the life of the ocean, it scarcely extended beyond paddling depth. Limited not only by that, but by the restricted vision of the un-extended human eye (the microscope is several centuries into the future) – just as until the early seventeenth century our experience of celestial creation above the atmosphere was limited to what the eye could see without the fabulous extension provided by the telescope – our speculations about what ultimately lay behind and beyond and beneath it all could only be the lisping of a child in its conception of what that could possibly mean, spelt out in the syllables of intelligent apes, conjured out of human ideas of might and majesty (with the imaginative addition of such novel features as human creatures with long dresses and wings and a life after death spent beyond the clouds).

And perhaps the simple, beautiful words of the Angelic Doctor were adequate articulation of our thirteenth-century understanding of what God is about in creation. But nothing less than an endless symphony, sounded with all the harmony the advance of musical sensibility makes possible, will do in response to what the progress of modern biology allows us to see of the nature and genesis – and familial kinship – of life on earth, of which we are the chosen species in whose hands is placed the responsibility for its preservation and continuance.

Encounter

The deeper our appreciation, the closer we come to God's own delight in his embodiment in material being – if 'close' can ever be an appropriate adjective in discussion of our relationship with God. This appreciation is always in the first instance sensory and aesthetic, only subsequently enhanced – and immeasurably so – by the penetrative gaze and grasp of the intellect and spirit, its hold upon us making us aware of a longing deeper than deep within us for what is taking possession of us through this presence in our lives.

As our appreciation of the beauty and diversity of life grows, so does our understanding of the utter complexity of every other life form – that each of them is as physically, chemically and biologically complex as we humans are, each in its unique way. The more we study a particular group the more we are drawn into the thrill of its being whether it be moths, flowers, hoverflies, fishes, birds or snails. As you attend in this way you come to appreciate these beings as God appreciates them. Such attention is the very core of worship, and the gratitude that wells up in us is the very essence of Eucharist. 'This quality of seeing the world with attentive and loving care is profoundly religious,' writes Elizabeth Johnson.[26] The thrill I get is the faintest echo, the palest reflection of God's fulfilment in creation. And it comes to me though encounter with creation. Sensory encounter first of all, augmented and deepened by intellectual encounter. This is something that grows and develops through history.

When I immerse myself in this act of becoming acquainted more intimately with birds or flowers, mosses or spiders, at however far a remove, I experience the breath of the divine as fully as humanly possible. The deeper my intimacy grows the more I come to appreciate the inexhaustible nature of such experience and the more I sense how infinitesimal a portion of it any one person can embrace. It is so inexhaustible that it could not be plumbed even if everybody on earth embraced the privilege of peering into a corner of it.

The koan is not a literary form we associate with the literature of the West, but there are some examples.[27] One of the most profound is in the poetry of Tennyson:

Flower in the crannied wall,
I pluck you out of the crannies,
I hold you here, root and all, in my hand,
Little flower – but if I could understand
What you are, root and all, and all in all, I should know what
God and man is.[28]

'If I could understand,' Tennyson says, but all of us, in our various ways and to varying degrees, are like the Peter of Wordsworth's poem, *Peter Bell: A Tale in Verse*, about a man of limited sensibility, whose eyes are opened during the course of the narrative, but for whom to begin with:

A primrose by a river's brim
A yellow primrose was to him,
And it was nothing more.[29]

We don't see ourselves in the Peter of the poem's early stanzas; but then, when did you last meet someone who sincerely identified with the Pharisee rather than the Publican of Jesus' parable (Lk 18:9-14)?

Incarnation[30]

Just as there are intimations of evolution in the way people thought about creation much earlier than the nineteenth century, so too this new way of thinking about incarnation is presaged in earlier theological speculation. One of the foundational concepts of Neoplatonism, seen in a more developed Christian way in the writings of St Thomas, is that all the different forms of being we see in creation are embodiments of ideas in the mind of God. But in the mind of God they are perfect, the archetypes of the beauty to which we respond in creatures. It was part of the thinking of the philosophers who pondered the great chain of being that, God being what he is, every possibility would have to be realised, embodied in creation. Indeed, this conviction was behind the search to discover new forms and patterns and the deeper the search penetrates, the closer we come to an appreciation of the archetypes in the mind of God – or as close as it is possible for our human mind and body to do so.

And yet, in theology we are held fast in a formulation of what incarnation means that was welded together to still the speculative theological turmoil that was rife in 325 CE, even though that formulation is steeped in a child's grasp of what creation means. We are reminded of something Charles Raven wrote more than sixty years ago:

> **We as human creatures limited by our status cannot speak with knowledge of what transcends our experience: we may lay down certain propositions about the nature of the Godhead, we may support them by inference and analogy, but it is sinful pride, and great foolishness, to talk as if we could define the infinite or formulate absolute truth. We must beware of claiming for our words an ultimate wisdom, an inerrant authority.[31]**

It is worth emphasising again that the spark that inflames the tinder of our human thirst for God is our physical, emotional and intellectual encounter with creation in the first instance. The leap of recognition that finds expression in our joy at what we find there is the same for the spirit of a Stone Age man gazing at the sunset or at shoals of salmon swimming upstream to spawn, as it is for a modern man thrilling to the beauty of the Krebs cycle or the equations to which electrons dance, or the newly discovered intricacies of the lives of orchids or bats. And it is the search that matters, not the explanation we give of what we think we are doing in the sense of why we are doing it.

There is no substitute for this encounter. It might be thought that with the advance in technology, the stupendous increase in the sophistication and resolution of computers and imaging systems, and the advent of virtual reality, it can be substituted by forms of mediated experience. But such experience is entirely dependent on the natural world itself. Late in the nineteenth century the great Belgian scientist and explorer Jean-Charles Houzeau perceptively remarked that we encounter true novelty only in nature itself, 'our imagination, as powerful as it seems at first, is only rich in combination of things that are already known':

> The invention of the microscope and the telescope has therefore not just contributed in opening up a new world for us, so vast that we cannot yet appreciate its whole extent; it has also shown us the contrast between the character of our mental faculties and the richness of nature. We have there a palpable proof that imagination, as powerful as it seems at first, is only rich in the combination of things that are already known. It forms assemblages of great variety, often odd and monstrous; it knows how to amplify or to diminish its pictures in all proportions. But from its own depths it does not draw anything that is really new; and as inventive as it thinks itself it would find nothing if nature did not furnish the models.[32]

In the book of Job we hear in Job's final answer to God, 'Therefore have I uttered that I understood not; things too wonderful for me, which I knew not ... I have heard of thee by the hearing of the ear: but now mine eye seeth thee' (42:3, 5). And Josef Pieper in *The Silence of St Thomas* put it accordingly, saying:

The world in which man today leads his ordinary life is becoming more and more a purely technological one. The things with which he is concerned are artificial; they are artefacts, not creations. The danger inherent in this situation is that man might, erroneously, come to regard the world as a whole and the created things with it – above all, man himself – in the same manner in which he regards, correctly, his own artefacts belonging to the technological sphere; in other words, man is beginning to consider the whole world of creation as completely fathomable, fully accessible to rational comprehension, and above all, as something which it is permissible to change, transform, or even destroy.[33]

What is the nature of this something at the heart of the forms of creation that we respond to intuitively? St Thomas' word for it is its 'light', *Ipsa actualitas rei est quoddam lumen ipsius*: 'the reality of a thing is itself its light.'[34] But it is utterly beyond our capacity to know the source of that 'sound' in itself: 'We have no power of perceiving this correspondence by which the formal truth of things is constituted.'[35]

This harmony the Pythagoreans and their mathematical disciples in our own day understood in terms of proportion, of measure. The musician hears it as sound. It is 'heard' by the naturalist in what is seen and understood, and by all those who experience the consonance which is ecstasy, whether sexual or athletic, intellectual or spiritual. These are all different facets of the same something that is beyond sense or human understanding, but in which, in whom, all these are at once are embraced.

When we look at the beauty in all or any of its dimensions we do not see a reflection of a creator that is other, an absent artificer. We see – we experience – something of God. We are in the presence of God. I am *with* God. I am *in* God. And God is in me, as he is in the buttercup or the butterfly or the spider. My experience encounters and attempts to embrace. For Thomas each is an expression, an embodiment, shaped by matter and energy, of an aspect of the beauty of the creator: not merely a reflection in a mirror of some aspect of the divine.[36]

We must preface every attempt to speak of this with acknowledgement of the utter inadequacy of the words we must use to speak of it, most of all of the word 'God' itself. Creation is the embodiment of God. This is not to say creatures are God, who is other and beyond – though not in any spatial sense because dimensionality enters the picture only with the coming into being of material things. Creation is the appearance of God in materiality: the things of creation on the one hand and the unfolding process that is cosmic evolution on the other. When we respond to beauty, truth, joy, intelligibility in any facet of creation we are in tune with that something of God at the heart of it. No wonder we stumble over ourselves here in our attempts to find words that will fit. Something of God, but the tiniest scintilla, and touched only when we reach, heard only when we listen. We pick it up with our senses, with our mind, with our spirit. We may perhaps not recognise it for what it is if our reception is sensual only, or if it is emotional only, or only intellectual: we receive it through all that we are.

We still don't have a word for what we respond to at the heart of experienced reality, for what it is that catches us. Beauty, truth, harmony are aspects of the colour of it, but not the thing itself. We thrill to the manifestation of creatures, to what they present in themselves when we encounter them. At times, those rare times when we see with a greater clarity of receptivity, it can be heart-stopping. It is G.M. Hopkins' awe before the hovering kestrel:

My heart in hiding
Stirred for a bird, – the achieve of, the mastery of the thing.
Brute beauty and valour and act, oh, air, pride, plume, here

Buckle! AND the fire that breaks from thee, then, a billion
Times lovelier, more dangerous, O my chevalier![37]

It is the ecstasy of Alfred Russel Wallace's first encounters with the
butterfly *Ornithoptera Croesus*:

> The beauty and brilliance of this insect are indescribable, and
> none but a naturalist can understand the intense excitement
> I experienced when I at length captured it. On taking it out
> of my net and opening the glorious wings, my heart began to
> beat violently, the blood rushed to my head, and I felt much
> more like fainting than I have done when in apprehension of
> immediate death![38]

It is the excitement of Margaret Mee's vigil as she waits in darkness
for the blossoms of the Amazonian moonflower (*Selenicereus wittii*)
to open, 'transfixed by its spectral beauty and extraordinary sweet
perfume'.[39] It is the compulsion to fall to your knees at the shock
of seeing furze in riotous bloom for the first time, as Linnaeus is
reported to have done on his brief visit to England in 1736.[40] It
is my own, never-to-be-forgotten, heart-stopping amazement
at finding bee orchids for the first time when I was thirteen. So
overpowering is the response flowers can arouse in us that John
Ruskin refused to believe there could be anything functional about
their beauty, or if there was, it was surely secondary.

In nearly every major group there are species of comparable
sense-stopping beauty: wherever the possession of such a quality
is an important element of being what uniquely they are. Certain
groups are especially rich in such species. Among plants, orchids and
stapeliads most strikingly perhaps, but a visit to a botanic garden or
a trawl through the internet will show there are many other families
to rival these. Among animals, countless groups of insects and other

invertebrates, not to mention birds and mammals. In all such cases our appreciation is a fraction of that of the creatures at which this beauty is targeted: pollinating insects or birds in the case of flowers, other members of its own species in the case of birds and mammals.

But we might equally be overwhelmed by any other creature, if the angle of perception presented it in such a way that our human reception permitted comparable clarity of vision. This heart-stopping is the extreme of course. There is a spectrum of response, and where we are on that spectrum depends on our individual capacity, each of us differently endowed in this regard.

Nature is much more than the art of God. It is the embodiment of an artist who is otherwise incorporeal, immaterial. The materialisation of reality that is creation provides the medium through which God becomes visible. Something of God materialises in every species. In the words of D.H. Lawrence:

When from a world of mosses and of ferns
at last the narcissus lifted a tuft of five-pointed stars
and dangled them in the atmosphere,
then every molecule of creation jumped and clapped its hands:
God is born! God is born perfumed and dangling and with a little cup![41]

The Dimming of the Rainbow of Life on Earth

As we come to better understand God's purpose in creation in this light – the same light with which Thomas Aquinas saw it, but ours is a brighter light by far – it becomes clearer to us that creation is, at its most fundamental, about God's own self-fulfilment in being. It is not, therefore, for us or about us in the first instance, however central we are to its continuation into the future God intends. As we come to better understand God's purpose in creation in this light, we begin to see that the haemorrhaging of the living abundance and diversity of life we are bringing about in our time, the greatest ecological extinction the earth has ever experienced, has a significance that goes way beyond our concern for its impact upon our human welfare.

We evaluate the critical nature of the biodiversity crisis in terms of its effects on the human situation. But now that we are beginning to see the living earth as the very embodiment of divine purpose, everything in that human-centred perspective changes. This dimming of the rainbow of life's diversity is not merely inconvenient, but also potentially disastrous. It is denial of God's purpose. If we truly believe, and bring our understanding to bear upon what we are making of the world, we should be horrified. God's mind and heart and word to us are in all the species that weave life's diversity. Just as we look back appalled at the venality and cruelty of the advance of Christianity over the centuries, so (a thousand years into the future) we may look back on our moment of custodianship of the earth as the time we lost our way again.

The earth is given to us and it is our unique privilege and responsibility to care for it, not as we would care for a garden in which we grow the vegetables that sustain us but because it is the garden God walks in and we have been invited to walk with him. We are placed in this Garden of Eden to share in God's own wonder and delight at his creation. We alone are endowed with that gift of mind that enables us to tend and nurture it as God wants us to tend it.[42]

If we can attain this way of seeing in all of reality the manifestation of God, our relationship with creation – and with all the particular existents in which it is embodied – must be characterised essentially by fundamental reverence. It cannot be merely instrumental. This is the mysticism to which we are, all of us, called. We find an intuitive sense of it in primitive religions, which see in nature something numinous, whether identified with the things of nature themselves – trees, streams, mountains – or distinct from them, sometimes assuming personality and the mantle of divinity on some level. Our reverence is informed by our vastly greater understanding of how they have come to be, of how their history is entwined with ours, of the wondrous complexity whereby their existence is maintained.

When I step over the threshold I am in that presence. If I can clear my mind of the clutter of distracting thought, I free myself of things that prevent it sinking into me, and allow myself to redirect my sensory awareness of what is around me to the beings through which and in whose (lesser) presences this greater presence is mediated. This is the essential core common denominator of spiritual experience, prior to thought or word. It is the seed that crystallised in the rational mind all those tens of thousands of years ago, whose slow and progressive growth over the ages draws us forward, into a future where what is essentially human in us will come to the centre.

Part of that process of progressive crystallisation is the redirection of thought to the beings about us, through which we become in time overwhelmed by the awe of their achievement. This is the essential contribution of natural history, endless and myriad-faceted, to the growth and maturation of spirituality. And while it may appear that its end is knowledge per se, that knowledge is but the medium that takes us beyond itself to its source, 'The highest that we can attain to is not Knowledge, but Sympathy with Intelligence ... Nature is a personality so vast and universal that we have never seen one of her features.'[43]

On several occasions Pope Francis calls for 'profound ecological conversion'. The phrase is lightly skipped over but it is not lightly meant. There is no aspect of the encyclical where the depth and extent of that profundity is more likely to be underappreciated. Conversion is a metamorphosis of meaning, and in no other facet of the conversion called for here is this more demanding or more difficult to get our heads and our hearts around than the true meaning of life on earth. It is not accomplished in a flash. It is not something that is effected once and for all by being struck from the horse of our complacency, but merely initiated by that dawning of new insight. It must grow in us from there, in me as an individual over my lifetime, in the community in which we hold each other's hands on this new path we can scarcely see, in humanity at large on this pilgrimage into a distant future where, as only faith can comfort us, on some level deeper than our understanding can compass, the lion will lie down with the lamb and all tears will be wiped away.

But in the practice of our everyday spiritual lives it gives new meaning to the conservation and restoration of biological diversity. It provides us with an agenda within which our new awareness is nurtured and advanced. It has the advantage of being a secular agenda which we can share with the broader community and in the process perhaps advance ecumenical understanding in a way the narrower focus of the churches in this direction might otherwise fail to do.

What this involves will vary from place to place, but its territorial focus should be the parish; perhaps beginning with a new inventory and assessment of its natural diversity.

Endnotes

1. Unknown ninth- or tenth-century Irish author, in W. Stokes, *The Martyrology of Óengus the Culdee*, London: Henry Bradshaw Society, 1905, p. 56; printed (no. 234) in K.H. Jackson (trans.), *A Celtic Miscellany*, London: Penguin Books, revised edition 1971, p. 296. The 'Life' of Molua probably dates to the early twelfth century.

2. C. Plummer, *Vital Sancturum Hiberial*, 1910, 1. Translation is the author's own.

3. Gn 1:26; as also Gn 1:28: 'And God blessed them, and God said unto them, Be fruitful, and multiply, and replenish the earth, and subdue it; and have dominion over the fish of the sea, and over the fowl of the air, and over every living thing that moveth upon the earth.'

4. Quoted in Dermot Moran, 'Towards a Philosophy of the Environment' in J. Feehan (ed.), *Educating for Environmental Awareness*, Dublin: University College Dublin Environmental Institute, 1997, 2005, pp. 45–67.

5. Joseph Rickaby, *Moral Philosophy of Ethics and Natural Law*, London: Longmans, 1901, p. 199.

6. *Catechism of the Catholic Church*, London: Geoffrey Chapman, 1994, 299, 2415. See Andrew Linzey, *Creatures of the Same God: Explorations in Animal Theology*, New York: Lantern Books, 2009.

7. John Ray, *The Wisdom of God Manifested in the Works of Creation*, 1826, Ray Society facsimile reprint (2005) of the definitive Dove Edition of 1826; first published 1691.

8. Charles E. Raven, *John Ray: Naturalist: His Life and Work*, Cambridge: Cambridge University Press, 1942, p. 467.

9. *Life and Letters* II, p. 219.

10. John Ray, *The Wisdom of God*, pp. ix–x.

11. 18,000 plants, 150 'beasts', 500 birds, 500 fishes 'secluding shell-fish', 'but if the shell-fish be taken in, more than six times the number'; and 20,000 insects. John Ray, *Wisdom of God*.

12. Ibid., p. 24.

13. Donald Culross Peattie, *Flowering Earth*, 1948, Scientific Book Club edition, p. 46.

14. R.S.K. Barnes (ed.), *The Diversity of Living Organisms*, Oxford: Blackwell Science, 1998.

15. Lynn Margulis and Karlene Schwartz, *Five Kingdoms: An Illustrated Guide to the Phyla of Life on Earth*, New York: Freeman, 1998.

16. Among other key passages in *Laudato Si'* are the following: 'The ultimate purpose of other creatures is not to be found in us. Rather, all creatures are moving forward with us and through us to a common point of arrival, which is God' (83); 'Saint John of the Cross taught that all the goodness present in the realities and experiences of this world "is present in God eminently and infinitely, or more properly, in each of these sublime realities is God"' (234); Creation is 'a precious book, "whose letters are the multitude of created things present in the universe" [Quoting John Paul II]' (85); The Japanese bishops write of how every creature sings 'the hymn of its existence' (85).

17. In the prayer for the earth at the end of the encyclical God is addressed as 'present in the whole universe and in smallest of your creatures'. See 'Consider this Leaf' in *The Dipper's Acclaim and Other Essays*, Dalgan Park: The Columban Ecological Institute, 2016.

18. John Feehan, *Creation, Evolution and Faith: Reflections on the Presence of God in Creation*, Dublin: John Feehan, 2015, p. 7.

19. See Richard Dawkins, *An Ancestor's Tale*, London: Weidenfeld & Nicolson, 2004.

20. E.L. Grant-Watson, *Wonders of Natural History*, London: Pleiades Books, 1938, p. 192.

21. The *Summa* was written between 1266 and 1273.

22. Albert the Great (*c*.1260), *Man and the Beasts: De Animalibus, Books 22–6*, trans. James J. Scanlan, New York: Medieval and Renaissance Texts and Studies, 1987. If we exclude Noah's inventory for the ark!

23. 477 numbered species: 113 quadrupeds, 114 flying animals, 140 swimming animals, 61 crawling animals and 49 'vermes'. Albert the Great, *Man and the Beasts*, p. 16.

24. 'My Brothers, we begin with the most important thing of all to us, our faith in God. About God we believe what he himself has revealed to us: that he is one, existing as the Trinity of Father, Son and Holy Spirit, infinite and eternal, utterly vast, yet present to even the smallest creature; he is both immeasurably far off and inconceivably close. Believing this gives us enough to live the life of Faith.

How arrogant it would be to seek to know God's inner secrets, mysteries of his life power and way of existence. And how futile! Our small minds are not made for that. Think of this world our familiar earth and sea: familiar indeed, and how much we know of them, and how little. What do we know of the teeming life beneath the waves, or even on much of the surface of the earth?' 'Sermons of St Columban' in *Sancti Columbani Opera*, G.S.M. Walker (ed.), *Scriptores Latini Hiberniae*, Volume II, Dublin: School of Celtic Studies, Dublin Institute for Advanced Studies, 1957.

25. *Summa Theologiae*, Ia, q. 47, a. 1. See also *Summa Contra Gentiles*, II, XLV.

26. Elizabeth A. Johnson, *Ask the Beasts: Darwin and the God of Love*, London: Bloomsbury, 2015, p. 41.

27. A koan is a Zen Buddhist riddle used to focus the mind during meditation, and to develop intuitive thinking.

28. Alfred, Lord Tennyson, 'Flower in the Crannied Wall', 1863.

29. William Wordsworth, *Peter Bell: A Tale in Verse*, London: Longman, 1819.

30. 'Those of us who are theologically inclined may wish to reflect on the way all of this deepens and extends the meaning of incarnation' (*Reflections on the Presence of God in Creation*, pp. 21–2); for the background see Niels Gregersen, *Incarnation: On the Scope and Depth of Christology*. Minneapolis: Fortress Press, 2013; and 'The Cross of Christ in an Evolutionary World', *Dialog: A Journal of Theology*, 40, 2001, pp. 192–207.

31. Charles E. Raven, *Experience and Interpretation. The second series of the 1951–2 Gifford Lectures: Natural Religion and Christian Theology*, Cambridge: Cambridge University Press, 1953, p. 102.

32. J.C. Houzeau, *Bull. Séances Soc. Belge Microscopie*, 1887, quoted in E.F. Linssen, *Nature Interludes: A Book of Natural History Quotations*, London: Williams and Norgate, 1951, p. 239.

33. Josef Pieper, *The Silence of St Thomas: Three Essays*, South Bend, IN: St Augustine's Press, 1953, p. 92.

34. Commentary on the *Liber de Causis*, I. 6 in Josef Pieper, The Silence of St Thomas, p. 59.

35. Josef Pieper, *The Silence of St Thomas*, p. 59.

36. John Feehan, *Creation, Evolution and Faith*, pp. 16–17.

37. G.M. Hopkins, 'The Windhover', *Gerard Manley Hopkins: Poems and* Prose, London: Penguin, 1953, p. 30.

38. Quoted in Richard Mabey, *The Cabaret of Plants: Botany and the Imagination*, London: Profile Books, 2015, Ch. 27.

39. Alfred Russel Wallace, *The Malay Archipelago*, London: Macmillan, 1867.

40. The story is probably apocryphal. See J. Feehan et al., *The Bogs of Ireland: An Introduction to the Natural, Cultural and Industrial Heritage of Irish Peatlands*, Dublin: Dublin Environmental Institute, UCD, 1996, pp. 222–3.

41. D.H. Lawrence, 'God is Born'.

42. John Feehan, *Creation, Evolution and Faith*, p. 22.

43. Henry David Thoreau, *Walking*, Auckland: The Floating Press, 2009.

Laudato Si': Mining the Meanings for the City

MICHAEL PUNCH

Drawing on my own field of expertise and research interests, not to mention my adult life experience, I would like to offer some reflections on the urban content and implications of *Laudato Si'*. To do so might at first glance seem counter-intuitive since the encyclical has been seen principally as an environmental work with a strong emphasis on climate change. Indeed, the subheading 'On Care for our Common Home' would seem to confirm just such a central focus. Sadly, we have been bequeathed with an unhelpful dualistic social imaginary, which tends to equate environmental issues with rural contexts, and to see the urban as somehow an entirely separate concern. We need to guard against this habitual separation of society and nature.[1] The cultural critic Raymond Williams argued convincingly that we need a renewed 'structure of feeling' connecting nature and the city.[2]

Specifically, this chapter will consider how the city in its neoliberal manifestation of recent years has been arguably ill-served by a flawed analysis and policy regime. The neoliberal city is one wherein the direction of policy has been increasingly steered by cost-benefit calculations rather than missions of service, equity and social welfare.[3] The chapter attempts to explore how a process of ontology, which is suggested by *Laudato Si'*, would help us to arrive at a more progressive analysis and policy regime, wherein the city could be reimagined and then remade to serve its people. The particular example of urban renewal projects is interrogated briefly from this perspective, focussing in passing on the example of the Dublin docklands regeneration.

The urban environment is often forgotten in the literature on 'global' problems such as climate change, deforestation, desertification, and species extinction – the last a problem poetically invoked in the encyclical:

> Because of us, thousands of species will no longer give glory to God by their very existence, nor convey their message to us. We have no such right. (33)

There is a cognate gap in much urban literature that neglects the physical environmental foundations on which the urbanisation process rests. A great deal of the urban theory is overtly sociological, failing to take account of physical or ecological processes. Could it be that Pope Francis indicates a method to redress some such imbalances? In particular, we should reflect on his repeated insistence that we notice how everything is connected:

> Everything is connected. Concern for the environment thus needs to be joined to a sincere love for our fellow human beings and an unwavering commitment to resolving the problems of society. (1)

There are several strong urban themes contained within *Laudato Si'*, as well as a powerful analytical approach, which can usefully help in how we reflect on the city and on how we live in the city. As noted, Pope Francis works with an ontology which sees everything as related, everything as interconnected (117, 142). We are many and our differences are great, but we share dignity in equal measure (90). We are all moments in a common relational process, an orientation that recalls the process theology of Alfred North Whitehead.[4] This approach emphasises becoming (process) and belonging (relationality), imagining the world 'as a living organism, a community of relationships in the process of growth and development'.[5] It follows that 'all modes of reality – natural, urban, or whatever – are distinguished by internal relations and interconnections'.[6]

This has considerable relevance to how we approach urban analysis and in practical terms on how we live in the city. Indeed, it echoes a central analytical tradition in geography and sociology, which insists we see everything as connected. The renowned urban geographer David Harvey suggests we need to approach urban space dialectically as a unified relational process consisting of many and complex related entities.[7] These are constantly 'becoming' through conflict and tension to form the apparent permanence of the received city. In a similar vein, the deep relational nature of all entities is central to this encyclical. Drawing on this interconnectedness, Pope Francis affirms the integral ecology of humanity and all creation. He notes that everything is interconnected, including time and space, and indeed atoms or subatomic particles. All life is part of a network that we will never fully explore or understand. We are part of nature, and living things have a value of their own in God's eyes; all creatures have their own purpose.

On this note, the Pope affirms a strong sacramental view of creation: 'soil, water, mountains – everything is, as it were, a caress of God.' That everything is interconnected is central to the prescriptive comment too:

> There can be no renewal of our relationship with nature without a renewal of humanity itself. There can be no ecology without an adequate anthropology. (118)

Speaking on the decline in the quality of human life, Pope Francis notes the disproportionate and unruly growth of many cities (44), leading to spaces unhealthy to live in, 'not only because of pollution caused by toxic emissions but also as a result of urban chaos, poor transportation, and visual pollution and noise' (44). Yet, he also notes the close interconnection between urban spaces, memory and meaning. This signals a critical line of discussion with regard to urban renewal. Too often, strategies to 'renew' urban quarters succeed only in wiping out vibrant historic city quarters. There have been many grass-roots struggles over urban renewal programmes internationally; those involved in these struggles aim to assert the meaning and identity of urban spaces from the community perspective in the face of powerful, often destructive, forces of state and private capital.[8]

There are telling analytical emphases in the encyclical, which are of note for how we do urban analysis. We must refuse the tendency to 'turn reality into an object simply to be used and controlled' (11). The understanding we require is much more than intellectual appreciation or 'economic calculus' (11). We are not well served by the dominant technocratic paradigm (101) or indeed by neoliberal economic models. Pope Francis refers to those whose actions, if not words, reveal 'no interest in more balanced levels of production, a better distribution of wealth, concern for the environment and the rights of future generations', and goes on to comment:

Their behaviour shows that for them maximising profits is enough. Yet by itself the market cannot guarantee integral human development and social inclusion. (109)

Such neoliberal tropes are among the 'dysfunctional values which underpin our present economic system ... The church should challenge our earth-consuming culture and unmask the contemporary idols which are seducing many people and fostering untold pain, exploitation and destruction.'[9]

Along with this ontological approach, there are strong normative lines of argument contained in the encyclical which can reorientate how we do urban analysis and indeed how we live in the city in peace and solidarity. Pope Francis argues for the connection between 'care for the vulnerable and an integral ecology lived out joyfully and authentically' (10). There is an integral link between 'concern for nature, justice for the poor, commitment to society and interior peace' (10).

Important analytical principles flow from these normative orientations, as an integral ecology calls for categories that 'transcend the language of mathematics and biology, and take us to the heart of what it is to be human' (11). The limits of the habitual language and the dominant mode of analysis become clear from this normative orientation. These ways of seeing and being can be usefully applied to the urban. Pope Francis is refusing to turn reality into an object simply to be used and controlled (11). This provides a solid basis to reject the tendency to commodify urban space; it resonates with Rasmussen's 'invitation to cultivate critical virtues of humility, care, awe and respect in a world ... worthy of so much more than the ransacked stage-and-storehouse made of it'.[10] This argument is echoed in the encyclical's understanding of the poverty of St Francis as 'something much more radical: a refusal to turn reality into an object simply to be used and controlled' (11).

Pope Francis insists on linking ecology to wider social-ethical concerns of society:

Concern for the environment thus needs to be joined to a sincere love for our fellow human beings, and an unwavering commitment to resolving the problems of society. (91)

Thus, 'peace, justice and the preservation of creation are three absolutely interconnected themes' (92) and 'hence every ecological approach needs to incorporate a social perspective, which takes into account the fundamental rights of the poor and the underprivileged' (93).

In *Laudato Si'* we are challenged to remember that 'all of us, as living creatures, are dependent on one another' (42) and that '[t]his experience of a communitarian salvation often generates creative ideas for the improvement of a building or a neighbourhood' (149). We could scarcely find a more powerful argumentative basis for the caring renewal of a living urban community – these people in this place, where identity and belonging are forged in specific streets and cherished built environments.

A central challenge for urban analysis implied by the normative and analytical orientation contained in the encyclical is to record and challenge the destructive socio-ecological experiences widespread within contemporary urban spaces. Cities today are marked by marginalisation, debasement, inequality, homelessness and gentrification. These imply experiences of injustice, displacement and loss. Consider a grass-roots critique of the Docklands regeneration project in Dublin, which emphasised the 're-awakening of the inner dimensions of our communal lives' over and above any physical master plan:

It is ironic that remote large corporations are increasingly reshaping the geography, architecture and social history of

the North Wall, with economic criteria the main arbiter of change. People, place, roots, heritage and culture are secondary considerations in the decision making process and require a determined DDDA (regeneration authority) to maintain such soulful considerations.[11]

It has been already noted that while the encyclical draws attention to problems of urbanisation ('disproportionate and unruly growth of many cities'; 'congested and chaotic neighbourhoods'), it also identifies the close connection between urban spaces, memory and meaning (84). This is a reality that should be central to how we respond to urban decay in renewal programmes, such as those operating in the Dublin docklands.

We should recall that the city is first a socio-environmental process, a constellation of events and related entities in a moment. The encyclical speaks to something of this urban reality by asking us to reflect on the foundational experience of playing outdoors in the neighbourhood square: going back to such places is to recover something of the essence, your true self (84). Every effort to protect and improve our world entails profound changes in 'lifestyles, models of production and consumption, and the established structures of power which today govern societies' (5). These are all elements in how our cities operate, as modes of production and consumption, and as spatial structures, which house and encourage particular ways of being and doing.

Endnotes

1. Nik Heynen, Maria Kaika and Erik Swyngedouw (eds), *In the Nature of Cities, Urban Political Ecology and the Politics of Urban Metabolism*, New York: Routledge, 2006.

2. Raymond Williams, *The Country and the City*, London: Chatto and Windus, 1973, p. 46.

3. Helga Leitner and Eric Sheppard, '"The City is Dead, Long Live the Net": Harnessing European Interurban Networks for a Neoliberal Agenda', *Antipode*, 34(3), 495–518, 2002.

4. Alfred North Whitehead, *Process and Reality*, New York: The Free Press, 1978.

5. Paul S. Fiddes, *The Creative Suffering of God,* Oxford: Clarendon Press, 1988, p. 39.

6. Joseph Grange, *The City: An Urban Cosmology*, New York: State University of New York Press, 1999, p. xvi.

7. David Harvey, *Justice, Nature and the Geography of Difference*, Oxford: Blackwell, 1996.

8. Manuel Castells, *The City and the Grassroots,* London: Edward Arnold, 1983.

9. Sean McDonagh, *Passion for the Earth: Christian Vocation to Promote Justice, Peace, and the Integrity of Creation*, London: Geoffrey Chapman, 1994, p. 124.

10. Larry Rasmussen, 'Drilling in the Cathedral', *Dialog: A Journal of Theology*, 42:3, 202–25, 2003.

11. Martin Byrne, *Walking Along With Docklands Mystics: The Changing Faces of North Wall's Christian Spiritualities*, Dublin: Elo Press, 1999, p. 18.

The Disruptive Power of
Laudato Si' – A 'Dangerous Book'

LORNA GOLD

Every revolution needs a unifying reference point. Ireland's rising had the 1916 Proclamation, Mao Zedong had his 'little red book' and the civil rights movement had Martin Luther King's 'I Have a Dream' speech. Each struggle against injustice, it seems, is encapsulated in a moment that pierces a hole in the prevailing logic. In the fight against climate change and environmental destruction, Pope Francis' encyclical has rapidly become that central rallying cry – and lays out a road map for a just and sustainable society.

The disruptive power of this 'little book' was evident in the days following its publication – and power has continued to grow. Global campaigner Bill McKibben, in his essay on *Laudato Si'* in the *New York Review of Book*, describes *Laudato Si'* as an 'event' rather than a book. 'The power of celebrity is the power to set the agenda, and his [Pope Francis] timing has been impeccable. On those grounds alone, *Laudato Si'* stands as one of the most influential documents of recent times.'[1] Naomi Klein, author and campaigner, highlights the way in which Pope Francis is 'overturning centuries of theological interpretation that regarded the natural world with outright hostility – as a misery to be transcended and an "allurement" to be resisted'.[2]

Not everyone agrees, however. The encyclical has been received by some in political circles, and even within the Church, with scepticism and even disdain. Sceptics within and outside the Church regard Pope Francis as having gone too far – entering into political questions rather than providing teaching which is based on 'sound theological analysis'.[3] In the days following the encyclical, Jeb Bush famously commented that he doesn't take his economic policy 'from my bishops or my cardinals or my pope'.[4] The point, however, is not simply whether the Pope was right or wrong – but the capacity of the message to throw open the most important contemporary debate in a way that would have been hitherto deemed unthinkable.

In the days following its publication, I found myself at a high level Vatican conference to reflect on the encyclical and the forthcoming climate talks.[5] As I wrote of the experience in a blog:

> It was quite a surreal experience. First I found myself introducing campaigner and activist Naomi Klein, as I chaired (possibly) the first ever all female panel at a high level Vatican conference. Later the same day, I was sitting on a bus beside former Irish President Mary Robinson and Kumi Naidoo of Greenpeace on our way to an open air Mass in an ancient pine forest. We were Catholics, Protestants, Jews, Muslims, atheists, feminists, liberals, conservatives, and everything in between. As the sun set over the beautiful pine trees, and the red full moon rose in the sky, the whole thing had a strange dream-like quality about it. There was an odd sense of being alive at a pivotal moment – giving praise to God, Allah, Yaweh, Mother Earth, the Force – with such an unlikely group of people.[6]

Looking back, I think what we all experienced was the disruptive power of Pope Francis' encyclical and its latent potential to 'bend the arc of history towards justice', as Martin Luther King famously said. Someone at the conference described the encyclical as 'the most dangerous book'. Others pointed out that many civil society organisations, whose very existence is based on speaking out against injustice, had been suddenly 'out radicalled' by the Pope.[7] Pope Francis had broken open the public debate by saying the unsayable. He offered a new vocabulary to express in concrete terms the world that many want to see. He gave permission to everyone to say what has to be said. In doing so, he disrupted well-positioned lines of defence and threw them into disarray. Former 'enemies' found themselves uniting and what seemed like insurmountable differences suddenly seemed small or irrelevant. The encyclical seemed to pulse with new possibilities. The reaction wasn't Pope Francis mania either. The group gathered at the Vatican conference, for example, were a very unlikely papal fan club. Such was the disruptive power of *Laudato Si'* – and its perfect timing – that it brought divergent views together for the greater good. It is a power that has not diminished over time, but has grown. New relationships have been forged and new alliances have emerged.

But what is the source of this power? The disruptive power of *Laudato Si'* derived partly from its author. A significant part of this power lay not only in the message, but in the power of the sender himself. In a world where celebrity drives culture, as Bill McKibben points out, Pope Francis was able to use his global celebrity status to drive a new agenda at a pivotal moment. The tone, however, was key to the receptivity of the message. Pope Francis presents what he sees as the Gospel truth, with all its raw beauty and its pain, in an uncompromising and compelling way. Yet the tone was far from dogmatic. It had the power to surprise. Here, suddenly, was a pope who didn't prescribe answers but set out his perspective on the state of the world and called on everyone to join with him in a groundbreaking act of dialogue. Moreover, his tone was preceded and followed by a coherent example: he sought to embody or 'live' his message of dialogue and servant leadership. In doing so, he became the de facto leader of a global 'countercultural' movement overnight and *Laudato Si'* became its 'little book'.

The Novelty of *Laudato Si'*

Many of the arguments Pope Francis makes in *Laudato Si'* regarding environmental and social disintegration are well rehearsed. Many climate scientists, economists and political leaders have been discussing these issues for decades. *Laudato Si'* in some respects has little new to say – as some commentators have rightly pointed out. The power of *Laudato Si'*, perhaps, also rests in this very fact. As a document, it doesn't seek to overturn established scientific facts or to prescribe a utopian future which is alien to the prevailing culture. Rather, it casts light on what science and life experience is already saying. It opens hearts to the 'cry' which is often hidden in the amassing of information. As Pope Francis says:

> **Our goal is not to amass information or to satisfy curiosity, but rather to become painfully aware, to dare to turn what is happening to the world into our own personal suffering and thus to discover what each of us can do about it. (19)**

It is about inviting everyone to take ownership of the planet's sufferings, in a way that is deeply involving, in an almost sacrificial way. The messenger empowers messages that are already known. This is perhaps why so many people who have fought and campaigned on issues as diverse as climate justice, homelessness, poverty, water privatisation, biodiversity loss and the rights of indigenous peoples all found themselves reflected in *Laudato Si'*. It reaffirmed their own knowledge and experience in a world that too often has chosen to be very selective in its ways of knowing.

There is, however, also a profound novelty in *Laudato Si'*. It lies principally in the synthesis itself – and its recognition of the inherent value in the capacity to form a new synthesis. Right from the outset, Pope Francis takes a different perspective. After reading it for the first time, I had the sense that engaging with *Laudato Si'* was like opening Google Earth and panning out far into space. Pope Francis brings a sense of wonder at existence, calling us back to a sense of awe at life on this fragile planet, stopping us in our tracks. In some ways, Pope Francis does for this generation what Copernicus did in the fifteenth century and the Apollo missions did in the 1960s: he restores our capacity to see the whole. He articulates in a new way the value of seeing the whole – and the dire consequences of our inability to grasp it.

The truth is that issues such as singularity, integration and synthesis are notoriously difficult to get your head around. Capturing the complexity of a whole system, a singularity, whilst honouring and respecting the complexity of the whole is as much an art as science. In *Laudato Si'*, he does not pretend to know it all. Instead, he paints a picture, a kaleidoscope of beauty and destruction which is messy, yes, but compelling. Knowing the whole is not to presume to understand all of the parts. This is perhaps Pope Francis' greatest insight, which he presents in a way that is both simple and compelling.

He recognises that synthesis and integration of perspectives are essential in tackling problems which are both environmental and human. The fragmentation of perspectives has resulted in knowledge systems that make decisions which are good or rational in one area (for example, economics), but which have detrimental consequences in another area (ecology). The knowledge economy has tended over several decades, perhaps centuries, to privilege certain knowledge bases over others – with the result that particular types of knowledge are taken as common sense. Pope Francis draws attention to the 'one-dimensional technocratic paradigm,' which in his view is pervasive, particularly in Western culture. He points out that this paradigm, which tends to recognise and value knowledge resulting from scientific method, is at best partial: there are other ways of knowing. Other truths exist and are essential to life. Even affirming this alone has the power to disrupt!

Our inability to integrate and synthesise has very real consequences, as Pope Francis points out. The absence of synthesis today is everywhere, especially in the political world. It results in incoherence in policies at every level and ineffective action. You can see this particularly when you go to the UN. It is remarkable to witness the sheer numbers and industriousness of NGOs, policy makers and officials, all fighting for very worthy goals – for the rights of people with disabilities, for indigenous peoples, for small island states, for people living in extreme poverty, and so on. However, everyone is so caught up in fighting their own corner that virtually no one is thinking about the sum of the parts, the systemic questions. The realities of these systematic questions are complicated and the power interests are great. The result is ineffective action, not seeing the wood for the trees.

Pope Francis goes even further. He highlights the fact that this fragmentation of knowledge systems, and the dominance of the technocratic paradigm, is not happening in a vacuum. It is happening in an unequal world where financial and economic interests are increasingly transnational – and are profoundly weakening the power of democratically elected governments. The technocratic paradigm is being increasingly driven by transnational forces of profit-seeking entities which conflate technological advance with profit and human progress. Pope Francis is not shy about the serious risk this poses to political life. He draws attention to the governance of key technological developments, which have given a small number of individuals with knowledge and money tremendous power. Given recent human experience of communism and Nazism, he concludes that this situation is 'extremely risky' (104).

Integral Ecology and 'New Humanism'

Pope Francis reiterates the need to focus on the whole and seeks to put a new vocabulary on that 'wholeness' throughout the encyclical. The chapter on integral ecology is the shortest in the encyclical. It raises the most questions and provides the least answers. It is, above all, a call to engage in dialogue and a new conversation. Pope Francis points merely to the types of conversations that need to happen – and the nature of the process of conversing.

He points to the need for a 'new humanism' to emerge, which counters the prevailing uni-dimensional logic based on profit seeking and technological development. Pointing to the need for universal principles and values to be affirmed, Pope Francis highlights human rights and solidarity with the poor. His primary concern in articulating a new humanism is to reaffirm the primacy of 'being' over 'being useful', whilst challenging the enormous injustices and inequalities which prevail in society.

In this respect, the Pope is challenging those engaged in politics and public life to rethink the *hierarchy of public values* which underpins governance structures and public policies. He is challenging policies which currently put unlimited economic growth based on extractivism above other dimensions such as ecology – consumption above conservation, private gain above the universal destination of goods. The prevailing definitions of progress in terms of national and global economic growth, even when that growth is predicated on the destruction of the planet we call home, represent a serious block to this. In the 'lines of approach' chapter he draws attention to the way that this counter-posing of positions throws light on the inadequacies of one knowledge system alone to articulate good solutions.

By starting with the whole, the big picture, Pope Francis is able to articulate priorities in a way that others have failed. His focus and resulting list of priorities, for example, is in stark contrast with the shopping list approach of the Sustainable Development Goals, with their seventeen priorities and one hundred and sixty-nine targets. He points, for example, to the need to 'progressively replace without delay' our dependence on 'highly polluting fossil fuels' (165). He challenges the global shift towards privatisation, particularly of water, calling for a shift towards a 'circular model of production' (22), as well as more democratic, participatory forms of governance.

Whilst calling for systemic change, he does not manufacture solutions – but points to the fact that shifting towards an integral ecology is 'by definition' a collective exercise. Enabling this collective exercise in itself involves the development of certain values, skills and behaviours which are often overlooked in a world that values individual technical expertise. This means breaking down the intellectual and political silos and finding a way to achieve new insights through shared knowledge. You start with a common vision – but need to work hard to find a common language. In some cases, it is an act of invention! This requires an ability to dialogue, to share perspectives, to listen, to try to engage and understand the other's perspective and appreciate what is good about it. It requires an ability to see that none of us has the whole truth, but many of us have partial truths. This assertion, and the numerous cogent illustrations in the encyclical, have far-reaching consequences, particularly in relation to interdisciplinary working.

From Feminism to Maternalism?

Whilst *Laudato Si'* has been praised in many respects for its unique viewpoint and power, some have critiqued it as a missed opportunity from a feminist viewpoint. Pope Francis does not attempt to reform or overturn any fundamental teachings on the role of women or on reproductive health – including the question of population growth as a cause of environmental harm. In her remarks in the conference following *Laudato Si'*, Mary Robinson highlighted this omission and called for a revision of the encyclical to recognise the role of women as being intrinsically linked to environmental factors. Some of this criticism may be valid, and the lack of reflection on this is clearly a gap.

In my view, however, *Laudato Si'* is far more feminist than any preceding Church document. The feminism, however, is not restricted to a narrow or reductionist definition of women and men and their respective roles. It carefully avoids any essentialisms of what it means to be a man or a woman. Rather, the entire perspective of Pope Francis rests on an intensely maternal and sisterly perspective of existence. It imbues and underpins every aspect of the encyclical. The whole encyclical, in fact, revolves around this opening sentence: 'Our common home is like a sister with whom we share our life and a beautiful mother who opens her arms to embrace us' (1). Miss that, and you miss the point. In fact, the image that best sums up the new viewpoint that Pope Francis is proposing is that of a mother feeding her newborn child. It is the image that best embodies the most fundamental, natural, intimate relationship of mutual love and dependency. It is the icon par excellence of the culture of care that Pope Francis calls for.

This image of mother and child – the first tender bond of intergenerational care – is the measure of the love we now need to save us from ourselves, and our children from the perils of climate change. The socio-environmental crisis today is quite literally a mother-child tragedy unfolding before us. In the Vatican conference following *Laudato Si's* publication, Prime Minister of Tuvalu Enele Sopoaga reminded us that thousands of children are already faced with an uncertain future as climate refugees. Rather than getting lost in useless arguing, above all we need to draw our children and grandchildren close to us and make them a solemn promise to do everything in our power to change course. US Secretary of State John Kerry's decision to bring his young granddaughter with him to the signing of the Paris Climate Agreement reflects this intergenerational promise. In fact, my main motivation to work against climate change and injustice is simply to be able to answer the questions of my children when they grow up: 'You mean you knew – so what did you do?'

Moreover, the encyclical theme of earth as our common home recalls something of a maternal perspective. In seeing the earth as a home, humans are called to become as one family. For many mothers all over the world, the running of a home is second nature. This is not to in any way deny the role of fathers or seek to stereotype the 'woman's place'. A maternal perspective tends to think about the family first, ensuring there is enough to go round. Extending something of that simple idea of being one family to the world would seem like a key that can unlock new ways to care for our shared home. The word 'economy', in fact, comes from the Greek word *oikonomia* which translates as 'household management' and is based on *oikos* 'house' and *nemein* 'manage'. Through reimagining the economy from the perspective of the home, maternal care, sisterhood and ubuntu, we can start to build a truly transformative vision.

Moreover, perhaps the encyclical's most profound and simple message is one of maternal love. Our earth is our 'beautiful mother', with whom we need a loving relationship to survive and thrive. We are simply realising we are not the masters of creation. The truth is that we utterly depend on Mother Earth; we are as helpless in the face of nature as a newborn child feeding from its mother's breast. We urgently need to feel that again. When that loving relationship with the mother is broken, the impact on the child is devastating, and often irreparable. Repairing that loving relationship once more is essential. That is a dangerous message to those who wield absolute power.

The Renewal of Interiority

To overcome the fragmentation, and rebuild that loving relationship with Mother Earth, we must look to the final chapter of *Laudato Si'* on spirituality and education. While the lines of approach provide some political priorities derived from an integral analysis, the centrality of spiritual and cultural renewal required is evident in the last chapter. The transition articulated by Pope Francis – which must reflect a renewed care for creation and the poor – can only be achieved through a change of heart, a new *valuing* of interiority. Right from the outset of the encyclical, Pope Francis affirms that such interiority 'cannot be dismissed as naïve romanticism, for it affects the choices which determine our behaviour' (11). Through his radical lifestyle choices, St Francis was not putting on some 'veneer of asceticism'. Rather, he was affirming something radical: 'a refusal to turn reality into an object simply to be used and controlled' (11); in other words, an object of profit. In the final chapter, Pope Francis completes the circle by emphasising the attitudes, beliefs and values that give rise to a shift in perspective and direction.

Once again, the tone is important. These don't appear as dogmatic dictates, but resonate profoundly with many philosophical and psychological perspectives, which highlight the link between good mental health, well-being and human happiness. Western culture traditionally has placed little value on interiority – or seen it as a duality – yet there is a gradual dawning that this inner world is essential to bringing about change. Rather than rejecting indications of a tendency towards wholeness, simplicity, presence as 'new age' or contrary to Christianity, he embraces them and articulates them as central to the renewal of Christian life: 'Living our vocation to be protectors of God's handiwork is essential to a life of virtue; it is not an optional or a secondary aspect of our Christian experience' (217). Moreover, he emphasises that this 'ecological conversion' which is integral to Christian life is not only a private, individualised affair but also requires a 'community conversion', a collective experience.

Rather than focussing on quick technical fixes, the key question for society has to be: what is the interior world, the thought systems, the values that sustain or undermine an integral ecology? A communitarian spirituality, which is attuned to dialogue and mutual understanding, in this regard, emerges a critical public good not only for Christians, but for the salvation of humanity from its current crisis. As Pope Francis attests, this renewed ecology, underpinned by a new interiority, will transform all aspects of life from our education system to our economy. It can only start from the personal, but needs to be supported particularly by Church communities. In fact, the flourishing of a counterculture which recognises the beauty and value of less is a profound paradox. It is a hard sell for those who have bought into the dominant technocratic paradigm with its emphasis on profit and material consumption. *Laudato Si'* invites us literally to open that door and, like St Francis, to go outside and rediscover the wonder of being alive. To look at our world, with all its tragic beauty, with childlike eyes. Pope Francis, in *Laudato Si'*, points us all in that new direction.

Endnotes

1. Bill McKibben, 'The Pope and the Planet', *The New York Review of Books*, 13 August 2015, nybooks. com/articles/2015/08/13/pope-and-planet/

2. Naomi Klein, 'A Radical Vatican?' *The New Yorker*, 10 July 2015, newyorker.com/news/news-desk/a-visit-to-the-vatican

3. R.R. Reno, 'The Weakness of Laudato Si', *First Things*, 1 July 2015, firstthings.com/web-exclusives/2015/07/the-weakness-of-laudato-si

4. *The Guardian*, 'Jeb Bush joins Republican backlash against pope on climate change', 17 June 2015, theguardian.com/us-newqs/2015/jun/17/jeb-bush-joins-republican-backlash-pope-climate-change

5. CIDSE, 'the CIDSE conference "People and Planet First: the Imperative to Change Course" called for urgent climate action and greater transformation in economics and lifestyles', 8 July 2015, cidse.org/articles/rethinking-development/the-cidse-conference-people-and-planet-first-the-imperative-to-change-course-called-for-urgent-climate-action-and-greater-transformation-in-economies-and-lifestyles.html

6. Lorna Gold, 'The Disruptive Power of a "Dangerous Book"', *Charity and Justice*, 4 July 2015, charityandjustice.net/2015/07/04/the-disruptive-power-of-a-dangerous-book/

7. Ben Phillips, 'NGOs get their courage back on inequality and climate (thanks to the Pope)', *Global Dashboard*, 2 July 2015, globaldashboard.org/2015/07/02/ngos-get-their-courage-back-on-inequality-and-climate-thanks-to-the-pope/

Laudato Si' and Social Justice

BRIGID REYNOLDS AND SEÁN HEALY

Laudato Si' is a challenging document with strong arguments showing why action is required on climate change. This action can take on many forms. Here we look at it from a social justice perspective.

What is Social Justice?

When asked for an explanation of justice we draw on the Christian understanding, which comes from the biblical tradition. For the people of the Bible, justice was seen in terms of relationship. Justice was understood as a harmony which comes from fidelity to right relationship: with God, people and the land. This is a harmony that comes from balance in relationships: people's relationships with each other, people's relationship with their environment and people's relationship with their Creator.

In the light of today's emphasis on the individual it is worth noting the stance of the biblical people. They never saw themselves as individuals; rather they regarded themselves as members of a family. Their communication with God was through the community. A characteristic element of this faith was concern for their neighbours, especially the poor and excluded in the society (Deut 14:29; 15:7–9; Ex 22:21–2; Job 29:11–20; Prov 29:7).

The third partner in these biblical relationships was the land and natural resources. For many years they were a landless people, a nomadic population. They desired the security and identity that land could give. In view of this history it is not surprising that they had a great respect for the land and understood their role to be that of good stewards of God's creation. The fruits of this creation were intended to benefit all (Lev 25; Deut 15:1–23, 33:13–16; Neh 9:33–7; Prov 28:18–22; Jer 12; Am 8:1–12).

In *Laudato Si'*, Pope Francis provides a new, refreshing and challenging reminder of this biblical tradition with its emphasis on harmony in relationships. He also notes the disruption that has occurred. He acknowledges that we Christians have at times incorrectly interpreted the scriptures and he rejects the notion that we have been given dominion over the earth and over other creatures:

> The creation accounts in the book of Genesis contain, in their own symbolic and narrative language, profound teachings about human existence and its historical reality. They suggest that human life is grounded in three fundamental and closely intertwined relationships: with God, with our neighbour and with the earth itself. According to the Bible, these three vital relationships have been broken, both outwardly and within us. This rupture is sin. The harmony between the Creator, humanity and creation as a whole was disrupted by our presuming to take the place of God and refusing to acknowledge our creaturely limitations. This in turn distorted our mandate to 'have

dominion' over the earth (cf. Gen 1:28), to 'till it and keep it' (Gen 2:15). (66)

'Tilling' refers to cultivating, ploughing or working, while 'keeping' means caring, protecting, overseeing and preserving. This implies a relationship of mutual responsibility between human beings and nature. Each community can take from the bounty of the earth whatever it needs for subsistence, but it also has the duty to protect the earth and to ensure its fruitfulness for coming generations. (67)

A theme underpinning *Laudato Si'* is that all things and all creatures are connected, all are dependent on one another (42, 92, 240) and we are all called to manage and nurture this interconnectedness. Francis outlines the many disruptions that have occurred in these relationships over the centuries and the effects on 'our common home'. He calls us 'to hear both the cry of the earth and the cry of the poor' (49). He appeals to us 'to protect our shared home'. Noting that young people demand change, he goes on to say:

> They wonder how anyone can claim to be building a better future without thinking of the environmental crisis and the sufferings of the excluded. (13)

Francis highlights the damage being done to the environment, including climate change through global warming, pollution, quality of water, loss of biodiversity. He directly links the damage done to the natural environment to the damage being done to the human population. He calls us to integrate questions of justice into debates on the environment.

> The human environment and the natural environment deteriorate together; we cannot adequately combat environmental

degradation unless we attend to causes related to human and social degradation. In fact, the deterioration of the environment and of society affects the most vulnerable people on the planet: 'Both everyday experience and scientific research show that the gravest effects of all attacks on the environment are suffered by the poorest'. For example, the depletion of fishing reserves especially hurts small fishing communities without the means to replace those resources; water pollution particularly affects the poor who cannot buy bottled water; and rises in the sea level mainly affect impoverished coastal populations who have nowhere else to go. The impact of present imbalances is also seen in the premature death of many of the poor, in conflicts sparked by the shortage of resources, and in any number of other problems which are insufficiently represented on global agendas. (48)

These observations and analyses of *Laudato Si'* challenge us to see the bigger picture and take our share of responsibility for global realities. As we grow to maturity, our education and socialisation systems make us aware of the justice dimension of our face-to-face and community relationships. Adulthood means that we go further and that we affirm the interconnectedness of all people, creatures and things on the planet. It demands that we accept this connectedness and that we nurture these relationships. We relate indirectly to all people and the environment through a variety of structures and accords.

Structural Dimensions of Social Justice

Justice demands that we look at the structural dimensions of our relationships. These relationships are conducted through a number of institutions. As societies have developed, the number and complexity of institutions have increased. We relate to other people through these institutions. We need to become more sensitive and aware of the activities of these institutions and how they are affecting people and the environment. We support these institutions through our government structures and taxes. There is an onus on us to question the activities of these institutions and corporations and their effects on the harmony of creation.

In a limited way, we in Ireland have become conscious of the effects of institutional relationships over recent years as the European Union (EU) and its various institutions have been developing. One of the concerns was and is that small communities like Ireland might be marginalised or forgotten by the various institutions of the EU. This very legitimate concern should be accompanied by an equal concern that European institutions might use their power to oppress weaker, more vulnerable peoples and sensitive environments. This concern should also stretch to other international organisations with which we are affiliated and also to the various international agreements of which we are signatories.

These institutions and corporations take on a life of their own far removed from the problems they are causing. For example, a 1 per cent rise in bank interest rates in the developed world can result in millions of dollars being extracted from countries in the Global South. Very often people making these decisions don't think about who has to pay. Even though these decision makers don't look to the consequences, they are in a very significant relationship with the people who have to pay. Similarly, companies who dump toxic materials in the seas ignore the consequent destruction of aquatic life forms and the effects on neighbouring coastal communities.

Francis explains it thus:

This is due partly to the fact that many professionals, opinion makers, communications media and centres of power, being

located in affluent urban areas, are far removed from the poor, with little direct contact with their problems. They live and reason from the comfortable position of a high level of development and a quality of life well beyond the reach of the majority of the world's population. This lack of physical contact and encounter, encouraged at times by the disintegration of our cities, can lead to a numbing of conscience and to tendentious analyses which neglect parts of reality. (49)

Living justly, then, is about living in right relationship with people, institutions, environment and the Creator. As societies have grown in complexity there is a need for structures that facilitate just living. A just society is one that is structured in such a way as to promote right relationships so that human rights are respected, human dignity is protected, human development is facilitated and the environment is nurtured and protected.

A Question of Paradigms

If a just society along these lines is to emerge, if the common home we all share is to be saved and renewed for this and future generations, then our basic guiding paradigm must change from the current dominant 'technocratic paradigm' (106–114).

What is a paradigm? Fritjof Capra, author of the bestselling classic *The Tao of Physics* and co-author of *The Systems View of Life*, described a paradigm as 'a constellation of concepts, values, perceptions, and practices shared by a community, which forms a particular vision of reality that is the basis of the way the community organises itself'.[1]

Paradigms are extremely powerful as they determine one's world view. They underpin decisions concerning what constitutes a problem, how it should be approached, what action should be taken and what the desired outcomes might be.

A major paradigm shift occurred in the seventeenth and eighteenth centuries as a result of the scientific discoveries of the time. The world view moved from an organic to a mechanistic one. Nature (including the person) was seen as the perfect machine, composed of distinct parts and governed by exact laws. However, there was no measurement to show that the whole was greater than the sum of the parts. Only what could be counted mattered. This mechanistic paradigm has been aggravated by recent developments in technology.[2]

Pope Francis acknowledges the positive outcomes of this paradigm shift, for example, 'when technology is directed primarily to resolving people's concrete problems, truly helping them live with more dignity and less suffering' (112). However, Francis also alerts us to the fact that 'science and technology are not neutral' (114) and that people should resist being controlled by the technology and losing sight of the bigger picture.

> The specialisation which belongs to technology makes it difficult to see the larger picture. The fragmentation of knowledge proves helpful for concrete applications, and yet it often leads to a loss of appreciation for the whole, for the relationships between things, and for the broader horizon, which then becomes irrelevant. This very fact makes it hard to find adequate ways of solving the more complex problems of today's world, particularly those regarding the environment and the poor; these problems cannot be dealt with from a single perspective or from a single set of interests. (110)

Francis asks us to slow down, to look at reality in a new way and to move forward in a 'bold cultural revolution'. In the process we should 'appropriate the positive and sustainable progress which has been made, but also to recover the values and the great goals swept away by our unrestrained delusions of grandeur'. (114)

Property

Central to a more appropriate paradigm for the period ahead is the issue of ownership of property. The Christian tradition has a strong commitment to the common destination of goods. Pope Francis says:

> The Christian tradition has never recognised the right to private property as absolute or inviolable, and has stressed the social purpose of all forms of private property. Saint John Paul II forcefully reaffirmed this teaching, stating that 'God gave the earth to the whole human race for the sustenance of all its members, *without excluding or favouring anyone* ...' 'the Church does indeed defend the legitimate right to private property, but she also teaches no less clearly that there is always a social mortgage on all private property, in order that goods may serve the general purpose that God gave them'. (93)

This teaching has a long history. In the fourth century John Chrysostom, while recognising the right to private property, looked upon the wealthy as the stewards of God's creation. He wrote in his 'Homily on Lazarus' that 'the rich are in the possession of the goods of the poor, even if they have acquired them honestly or inherited them legally'. This statement has a lot to say to us today as we reflect on recent research that shows that the richest 1 per cent of people in the world own 48 per cent of global wealth, leaving just 52 per cent to be shared by the other 99 per cent. If present wealth share trends continue, by 2016 the top 1 per cent will have more wealth than the other 99 per cent (*Wealth: Having It All and Wanting More*, Oxfam, 2014). This inequality in the ownership of the earth's resources is the result of legal arrangements which favour small elites who use their current positions to ensure their privileged status is maintained when future agreements and accords are being designed and written into law.

Since everyone has a right to a proportion of the goods of the earth, society is faced with two responsibilities regarding economic resources: firstly, each person should have sufficient access to what is required to live life with dignity; and secondly, since the earth's resources are finite, and since 'more' is not necessarily 'better', it is time that society faced the question of putting a limit on the wealth that any person or corporation can accumulate. Espousing the value of environmental sustainability requires a commitment to establish systems that ensure the protection of our planet. *Laudato Si'* challenges us thus:

We need to take up an ancient lesson, found in different religious traditions and also in the Bible. It is the conviction that 'less is more'. A constant flood of new consumer goods can baffle the heart and prevent us from cherishing each thing and each moment. (222)

Technology

One of the major contributors to the generation of wealth is technology. According to *Laudato Si'*, we currently face a major problem in 'the way that humanity has taken up technology and its development according to an undifferentiated and one-dimensional paradigm' (106). The technology we have today is the product of the work of many people through many generations. Through the laws of patenting and exploration, a very small group of people has claimed legal rights to a large portion of the world's wealth. Pope John Paul II questioned the morality of these structures. He said: 'If it is true that capital, as the whole of the means of production, is at the same time the product of the work of generations, it is equally true that capital is being unceasingly created through the work done with the help of all these means of production' (*Laborem Exercens*, 14). Therefore, no one can claim exclusive rights over the means of production. Rather, that right 'is subordinated to the right to common use, to the fact that goods are meant for everyone' (*LE*, 14).

This understanding has been developed in *Laudato Si'*. It notes that for many generations men and women constantly intervened in nature but in a way that was respectful of the possibilities offered 'as if from its own hand'. It goes on to articulate how this reality has changed:

> Human beings and material objects no longer extend a friendly hand to one another; the relationship has become confrontational. This has made it easy to accept the idea of infinite or unlimited growth, which proves so attractive to economists, financiers and experts in technology. It is based on the lie that there is an infinite supply of the earth's goods, and this leads to the planet being squeezed dry beyond every limit. It is the false notion that an infinite quantity of energy and resources are available, that it is possible to renew them quickly, and that the negative effects of the exploitation of the natural order can be easily absorbed. (106)

The document goes on to advise us that the 'technocratic paradigm' is not neutral and tends to dominate us by its internal logic. It also dominates the economic and political life of our societies.

> We have to accept that technological products are not neutral, for they create a framework which ends up conditioning lifestyles and shaping social possibilities along the lines dictated by the interests of certain powerful groups. Decisions which

may seem purely instrumental are in reality decisions about the kind of society we want to build. (108)

Adopting and living by a new paradigm, according to *Laudato Si'*, would require a fundamental change in values. It would, for example, require an end to the 'throw-away culture' and a reversal of the current decline in the quality of human life. It would also mean that priority was given to the common good and that the value of solidarity would be constantly in evidence. As we have just seen, it would have profound implications for our understanding of property and for the distribution of whatever is produced by technology.

Work

A new paradigm would also challenge our understanding of work. Almost all agree that people have a right to work. Pope Francis discusses the meaning of work and emphasises the importance of work for everyone:

> We need to remember that men and women have the capacity to improve their lot, to further their moral growth and to develop their spiritual endowments. Work should be the setting for this rich personal growth, where many aspects of life enter into play: creativity, planning for the future, developing our talents, living out our values, relating to others, giving glory to God. (127)
>
> Work is a necessity, part of the meaning of life on this earth, a path to growth, human development and personal fulfilment. (128)

Over the past century, work has come to mean that every person has a right to a job. If everyone in the world seeking a job did have access to a meaningful job then the right to work would be recognised in practice as well as in theory. However, full employment (in the sense that everyone who wanted it had a paid job with income and conditions that respected their human dignity) has not been achieved over the past century despite it being the main political priority of almost every government that has held office across the world in that period. In fact, unemployment remains persistently high. As time passes and the world's technological capacity continues to expand, full employment looks less and less likely across the planet.

How, then, can people's right to work be vindicated? Perhaps the meaning of the word 'work' needs to be reclaimed. A paid job is not the only work in the world. There is extensive work done across the planet – much of it unpaid – in the home, in the community, on developing oneself (through education, for example) or on contributing to the development of other people or communities. In recent decades, such work has been ignored in discussions about the future of work. As it isn't paid employment, it is not counted in economic data. This work, however, is real and meaningful and essential for the continuation of the human race and the environment. It should be recognised as such.

Income

For such an approach to have any impact on securing everyone's right to work it must be accompanied by another aspect of the required reform of the dominant paradigm: how income is distributed. Over the past century, the dominant paradigm saw income being distributed as payment for jobs, with social welfare/ security payments during temporary periods of unemployment. This was supplemented with a pension once a person reached a particular age. Given the fact that full employment has not been achieved and is unlikely to be achieved in the foreseeable future, an alternative approach is required, one that would ensure everyone would receive sufficient income to live life with dignity, irrespective of whether or not they had a job.

A basic income system would be one approach that would achieve this outcome. Such a system is possible and can be financed. So it could be considered as part of an overall redesign of the dominant paradigm being called for by Pope Francis in *Laudato Si'*.

Poverty and Inequality

The persistence of poverty is one of the great scandals of our world today. Despite the bounteousness of nature and the development of advanced technologies, poverty persists.

> **The exploitation of the planet has already exceeded acceptable limits and we still have not solved the problem of poverty. (27)**

Ireland's National Anti-Poverty Strategy (NAPS), published in 1997 and updated in 2007, adopted the following definition of poverty:

> **People are living in poverty if their income and resources (material, cultural and social) are so inadequate as to preclude them from having a standard of living that is regarded as acceptable by Irish society generally. As a result of inadequate income and resources people may be excluded and marginalised from participating in activities that are considered the norm for other people in society.**

That is a comprehensive description of poverty. It is about money, but it is not just about money; it is also about the resources needed for inclusion in the society of which we are a part. Pope Francis draws attention, for example, to issues such as water poverty, pointing out that:

> Water poverty especially affects Africa where large sectors of the population have no access to safe drinking water or experience droughts which impede agricultural production. Some countries have areas rich in water while others endure drastic scarcity. (28)

He goes on to address an issue that has been problematic in many parts of the world in recent years: the privatisation of water.

> Even as the quality of available water is constantly diminishing, in some places there is a growing tendency, despite its scarcity, to privatise this resource, turning it into a commodity subject to the laws of the market. Yet access to safe drinkable water is a basic and universal human right, since it is essential to human survival and, as such, is a condition for the exercise of other human rights. Our world has a grave social debt towards the poor who lack access to drinking water, because they are denied the right to a life consistent with their inalienable dignity. This debt can be paid partly by an increase in funding to provide clean water and sanitary services among the poor. But water continues to be wasted, not only in the developed world but also in developing countries which possess it in abundance. This shows that the problem of water is partly an educational and cultural issue, since there is little awareness of the seriousness of such behaviour within a context of great inequality. (30)

At another point he contrasts different approaches to how society addresses nature and the consequent development of inequality:

When nature is viewed solely as a source of profit and gain, this has serious consequences for society. This vision of 'might is right' has engendered immense inequality, injustice and acts of violence against the majority of humanity, since resources end up in the hands of the first comer or the most powerful: the winner takes all. Completely at odds with this model are the ideals of harmony, justice, fraternity and peace as proposed by Jesus. (82)

An economic model based on the ever-greater concentration of the world's wealth in the hands of a very small elite needs to be changed if there is to be a just society. This planet has sufficient resources to ensure everyone has what is required to live life with dignity. But the dominant economic model results in these resources being distributed very unequally, causing extensive poverty and inequality within countries and between countries.

We fail to see that some are mired in desperate and degrading poverty, with no way out, while others have not the faintest idea of what to do with their possessions, vainly showing off their supposed superiority and leaving behind them so much waste which, if it were the case everywhere, would destroy the planet. In practice, we continue to tolerate that some consider themselves more human than others, as if they had been born with greater rights. (90)

Political Action

If issues such as the protection of biodiversity, melting polar ice caps, increasing emissions of methane gas and carbon dioxide, the loss of tropical forests, the loss of species of animals and plant groups, the threat to water and to natural habitats, desertification and increased pollution (all named in *Laudato Si'*) are to be addressed, significant and appropriate action at a political level will be required. Pope Francis points to some successes, such as the 1992 Earth Summit in Rio de Janeiro, which he says was a real step forward and prophetic for its time; however, its recommendations have been poorly implemented.

Overall, he is very critical of the weak response from political leaders to the challenges the world currently faces, especially on ecological issues. He describes the Rio+20 summit documents as being wide-ranging but ineffectual (cf. 169). He says that 'the myopia of power politics delays the inclusion of a far-sighted environmental agenda within the overall agenda of governments' (178). He is critical of the approach of political leaders in better-off countries who address the difficult challenge of reducing carbon and methane emissions by buying carbon credits from poorer countries that have less emissions.

The strategy of buying and selling 'carbon credits' can lead to a new form of speculation which would not help reduce the emission of polluting gases worldwide. This system seems to provide a quick and easy solution under the guise of a certain commitment to the environment, but in no way does it allow for the radical change which present circumstances require. Rather, it may simply become a ploy which permits maintaining the excessive consumption of some countries and sectors. (171)

He points out that in the twenty-first century, while maintaining systems of governance inherited from the past, we are witnessing a weakening of the power of nation states chiefly because the economic and financial sectors, being transnational, tend to prevail over the political. He goes on to argue that:

it is essential to devise stronger and more efficiently organised international institutions, with functionaries who are appointed fairly by agreement among national governments, and empowered to impose sanctions. (175)

He sees a major role for non-governmental organisations and intermediate groups in this process of producing action at a political level. He argues that they 'must put pressure on governments to develop more rigorous regulations, procedures and controls'. (179) He states that:

> while the existing world order proves powerless to assume its responsibilities, local individuals and groups can make a real difference. They are able to instil a greater sense of responsibility, a strong sense of community, a readiness to protect others, a spirit of creativity and a deep love for the land. They are also concerned about what they will eventually leave to their children and grandchildren. (179)

Social Action

If change is to happen in any of the areas already discussed in this chapter then people, individually and in groups, will have to take action to promote these changes. Pope Francis makes a wide range of suggestions on what people might actually do. For example, he urges a change of lifestyle and suggests that consumer movements could be very effective:

> A change in lifestyle could bring healthy pressure to bear on those who wield political, economic and social power. This is what consumer movements accomplish by boycotting certain products. They prove successful in changing the way businesses

operate, forcing them to consider their environmental footprint and their patterns of production. When social pressure affects their earnings, businesses clearly have to find ways to produce differently. This shows us the great need for a sense of social responsibility on the part of consumers. Purchasing is always a moral – and not simply economic – act. Today, in a word, the issue of environmental degradation challenges us to examine our lifestyle. (206)

He goes on to make a wide range of specific recommendations concerning what people might do, such as:

[A]voiding the use of plastic and paper, reducing water consumption, separating refuse, cooking only what can reasonably be consumed, showing care for other living beings, using public transport or car-pooling, planting trees, turning off unnecessary lights, or any number of other practices. All of these reflect a generous and worthy creativity which brings out the best in human beings. Reusing something instead of immediately discarding it, when done for the right reasons, can be an act of love which expresses our own dignity. (211)

He also draws attention to the importance of changing mindsets if real change is to happen:

If we want to bring about deep change, we need to realise that certain mindsets really do influence our behaviour. Our efforts at education will be inadequate and ineffectual unless we strive to promote a new way of thinking about human beings, life, society and our relationship with nature. Otherwise, the paradigm of consumerism will continue to advance, with the help of the media and the highly effective workings of the market. (215)

Pope Francis shifts the focus to future generations, our children and grandchildren, to motivate people to work for long-term, sustainable change:

> Once we start to think about the kind of world we are leaving to future generations, we look at things differently; we realise that the world is a gift which we have freely received and must share with others. Since the world has been given to us, we can no longer view reality in a purely utilitarian way, in which efficiency and productivity are entirely geared to our individual benefit. Intergenerational solidarity is not optional, but rather a basic question of justice, since the world we have received also belongs to those who will follow us. (159)

Pope Francis sees this as an obligation of justice. He sees the environment as 'on loan to each generation which must then hand it on to the next' (159). An integral ecology is marked by this broader vision, according to Pope Francis.

Conclusion

Laudato Si' is a powerful and challenging document that goes to the heart of some of the biggest and most urgent issues that face our societies and our world today. It challenges everyone on this planet to face up to reality and to acknowledge that the climate is a common good, belonging to all and meant for all, but is now under serious threat. It strongly urges humanity to recognise the need for changes in lifestyle, in production and in consumption in order to combat global warming or at least the human causes which produce or aggravate it.

This is an encyclical that is about integral ecology, about the poor, about work, about the common good, about future generations.

At its core is a strong call for replacing the current dominant mechanistic and consumerist paradigm with a paradigm built on social justice and on right relationships.

It calls for political action and courage and acknowledges that taking up these responsibilities will inevitably lead to clashes between those advocating change and those with the mindset of short-term gain which dominates present-day economics and politics. Everyone has a responsibility in this situation. It is a time for courage, a time for taking selfless responsibility.

Endnotes

1.   Fritjof Capra, *The Web of Life: A New Scientific Understanding of Living Systems*, London: HarperCollins, 1996, p. 6.

2.   For further development on these and related issues cf. S. Healy and B. Reynolds, 'Progress, Paradigms and Policy' in S. Healy, and B. Reynolds (eds), *Social Policy in Ireland: Principles, Practice and Problems*, Dublin: Oak Tree Press, 1998.

Pope Francis on Power, Politics and the Techno-Economic Paradigm

PEADAR KIRBY

In an address to the World Humanitarian Summit in Istanbul in May 2016, President Michael D. Higgins called for 'a profound and integrated rethink of international politics, and of our theory and practice of economics, development and trade; it requires a reform of the representational structures of the world's peoples; and indeed it demands little less, I suggest, than a new paradigm of thought and action, grounded in a reconciliation between ethics, economics, ecology and cultural diversity'. This echoes one of many rich themes of *Laudato Si'*: 'A healthy politics is sorely needed, capable of reforming and coordinating institutions, promoting best practices and overcoming undue pressure and bureaucratic inertia' (181). Indeed, at the heart of the encyclical lies a radical and insightful exposure of the power realities of today's world, coupled with an inspiring vision of what, in *Evangelii Gaudium*, Pope Francis called the 'lofty vocation' of politics (205).

Myopia of Power Politics

There is a refreshing quality to the Pope's critique of 'the myopia of power politics' (178), both because it resonates with widespread perceptions and because it is so rarely acknowledged by those in leadership positions. Governments, he says, 'are reluctant to upset the public with measures which could affect the level of consumption or create risks for foreign investment' (178) so that 'the mindset of short-term gain and results ... dominates present-day economics and politics' (181). As a result, politics is often itself responsible for the 'disrepute in which it is held, on account of corruption and the failure to enact sound public policies' (197). The vacuum that results is often filled by business groups which 'in the guise of benefactors, wield real power, and consider themselves exempt from certain rules, to the point of tolerating different forms of organised crime, human trafficking, the drug trade and violence, all of which become very difficult to eradicate'. He goes on to say, 'If politics shows itself incapable of breaking such a perverse logic, and remains caught up in inconsequential discussions, we will continue to avoid facing the major problems of humanity' (197). Reflecting on the crisis of politics today, the Pope begins to identify some of its fundamental causes, stating: 'There are too many special interests, and economic interests easily end up trumping the common good and manipulating information so that their own plans will not be affected' (54).

The relationship between economic and political power, therefore, emerges as a subject to which Pope Francis devotes significant attention. 'Today, it is the case', he writes, 'that some economic sectors exercise more power than states themselves.' And, he goes on to say that 'economics without politics cannot be justified, since this would make it impossible to favour other ways of handling the various aspects of the present crisis' (196).

Yet, each seems to blame the other for poverty and environmental degradation:

> While some are concerned only with financial gain, and others with holding on to or increasing their power, what we are left with are conflicts or spurious agreements where the last thing either party is concerned about is caring for the environment and protecting those who are most vulnerable. (198)

Pope Francis affirms that 'politics must not be subject to the economy' and that instead 'there is an urgent need for politics and economics to enter into a frank dialogue in the service of life' (189). Without naming it as such, here the Pope seems to be addressing the neoliberalisation of politics, as public authority has been made subservient to the dictates of global markets, which political leaders are fearful of alienating. The concrete example he gives is telling and very pertinent to the Irish situation:

> Saving banks at any cost, making the public pay the price, foregoing a firm commitment to reviewing and reforming the entire system, only reaffirms the absolute power of a financial system, a power which has no future and will only give rise to new crises after a slow, costly and only apparent recovery. The financial crisis of 2007–8 provided an opportunity to develop a new economy, more attentive to ethical principles, and new ways of regulating speculative financial practices and virtual wealth. But the response to the crisis did not include rethinking the outdated criteria which continue to rule the world. (189)

This specific and concrete critique of the current dominant economic and financial policies followed by almost every country is quite remarkable for an authoritative papal document. It places

Pope Francis among the most radical critics of the power of finance in today's global order.

Techno-Economic Paradigm

While the ability of economic and financial power to trump political power is a valid critique – too rarely heard except from voices on the radical left that are easily dismissed in mainstream discourse – Pope Francis goes even further with his critique. It is this which, in my view, constitutes the most radical and original strand in this rich encyclical, exposing, in a way that is rare in public discourse, the fundamental power that structures society today. The topic finds its first mention in an astonishing, almost throw-away, comment. Lamenting the lack of culture and leadership to find new paths out of the present crisis, the Pope states:

> **The establishment of a legal framework which can set clear boundaries and ensure the protection of ecosystems has become indispensable; otherwise, the new power structures based on the techno-economic paradigm may overwhelm not only our politics but also freedom and justice. (53)**

Here the Pope is identifying a new power structure based on the techno-economic paradigm as a threat not only to the power of politics but, even more fundamentally, to our freedom and to justice itself. This constitutes a fundamental claim about today's world order that, if correct, is of enormous consequence. In the opening sentences of the next paragraph, he offers an illustration that, yet again, makes a most radical claim. It follows the frank and refreshing comment, 'It is remarkable how weak international political responses [to climate change] have been'. The Pope immediately ascribes responsibility for this weak response to the 'failure of global summits on the environment [to] make it plain that our politics are subject to technology and finance'. So, what was presented as a threat in the previous paragraph, now seems to be realised in the failures of the UN climate change process embodied in the UN Framework Convention on Climate Change (UNFCCC). The same paragraph goes on, 'The alliance between the economy and technology ends up sidelining anything unrelated to its immediate interests. Consequently the most one can expect is superficial rhetoric, sporadic acts of philanthropy and perfunctory expressions of concern for the environment, whereas any genuine attempt by groups within society to introduce change is viewed as a nuisance based on romantic illusions or an obstacle to be circumvented.' The techno-economic paradigm emerges, therefore, as a, if not *the*, fundamental obstacle to effective action on climate change. These astonishing claims from Pope Francis require further interrogation.

What is meant by the 'techno-economic paradigm'? This is elaborated on in a series of paragraphs at the beginning of the third chapter of the encyclical. Entitled 'The Human Roots of the Ecological Crisis', the chapter begins with sections on 'Technology: Creativity and Power' and 'The Globalisation of the Technocratic Paradigm'. The third and final section of this chapter is on 'The Crisis and Effects of Modern Anthropocentrism'. These section titles already link technology with humanity, particularly with an anthropocentrism that implies a link between the power of technology and the power of humans over the natural world. The reflection on technology begins with a positive recognition of the immense power of technology to improve the conditions of life (102, 104); however, a more questioning tone emerges when Pope Francis raises the issue of how wisely humanity is using this immense power, mentioning Nazism, communism and other totalitarian regimes: 'In whose hands does all this power lie, or will it eventually end up? It is extremely risky for a small part of humanity to have it' (104). The following paragraph goes further, opening up a very important line of enquiry that lies at the heart of the Pope's identification of the techno-economic paradigm as a major threat to humanity and an obstacle to addressing climate change adequately. The Pope begins by questioning the identification of technological development with progress, 'as if reality, goodness and truth automatically flow from technological and economic power as such'. A few sentences later, he makes the ominous assertions, 'Each age tends to have only a meager awareness of its own limitations. It is possible that we do not grasp the gravity of the challenges now before us.'

These reflections prepare the ground for the central point of the Pope's claims, as developed in the second section of this chapter. Significantly, he opens this by stating that 'the basic problem goes even deeper'. It concerns 'the way that humanity has taken up technology and its development according to an undifferentiated and one-dimensional paradigm', namely, setting up a seemingly confrontational relationship between humanity and nature. He illustrates this with the example of economic growth.

This has made it easy to accept the idea of infinite or unlimited growth, which proves so attractive to economists, financiers and experts in technology. It is based on the lie that there is an infinite supply of the earth's goods, and this leads to the planet being squeezed dry beyond every limit. (106)

It is characteristic of this pope that, instead of choosing an example that might be more widely acceptable, he chose the issue that constitutes the greatest heresy for all mainstream economists, namely that we have to begin questioning growth as the motor of our economies. We have now gotten to the core of the Pope's claims about the 'techno-economic paradigm'.

It can be said that many problems of today's world stem from the tendency, at times unconscious, to make the method and aims of science and technology an epistemological paradigm which shapes the lives of individuals and the workings of society. The effects of imposing this model on reality as a whole, human and social, are seen in the deterioration of the environment, but this is just one sign of a reductionism which affects every aspect of human and social life. We have to accept that technological products are not neutral, for they create a framework which ends up conditioning lifestyles and shaping social possibilities along the lines dictated by the interests of certain powerful groups. Decisions which may seem purely instrumental are in reality decisions about the kind of society we want to build. (107)

This technocratic paradigm 'tends to dominate economic and political life' (109), he writes, and 'tends to absorb everything into its ironclad logic', so that 'it has become countercultural to choose a lifestyle whose goals are even partly independent of technology, of its costs and its power to globalise and make us all the same' (108). This is a major obstacle to facing the deeper challenges raised by climate change: 'To seek only a technical remedy to each environmental problem which comes up is to separate what is in reality interconnected and to mask the true and deepest problems of the global system' (111). So dominant has it become that 'the idea of promoting a different cultural paradigm and employing technology as a mere instrument is nowadays inconceivable' (108).

A Bold Cultural Revolution

What is distinctive about the Pope's critique of the dominance of technological thinking in our age is that he never loses sight of the agency that drives it, namely 'the interests of certain powerful groups' (107). Thus, he links the economic and the technological, seeing the economic system and its priorities as being profoundly shaped by technology but the technology in turn being developed to further the interests of dominant economic groups. This allows him to stress the potential of human agency to live beyond the confines of the 'ironclad logic' of the techno-economic paradigm:

> Liberation from the dominant technocratic paradigm does in fact happen sometimes, for example, when cooperatives of small producers adopt less polluting means of production, and opt for a non-consumerist model of life, recreation and community. Or when technology is directed primarily to resolving people's concrete problems, truly helping them live with more dignity and less suffering. Or indeed when the desire to create and contemplate beauty manages to overcome reductionism through a kind of salvation which occurs in beauty and in those who behold it. An authentic humanity, calling for a new synthesis, seems to dwell in the midst of our technological culture, almost unnoticed, like a mist seeping gently beneath a closed door. (112)

Unusually, then, the critique of power leads Pope Francis to a strong affirmation of human agency, what he calls 'the urgent need for us to move forward in a bold cultural revolution'. This is a revolution that challenges the dominant technological paradigm.

> Science and technology are not neutral; from the beginning to the end of a process, various intentions and possibilities are in play and can take on distinct shapes. Nobody is suggesting a return to the Stone Age, but we do need to slow down and look at reality in a different way, to appropriate the positive and

> sustainable progress which has been made, but also to recover
> the values and the great goals swept away by our unrestrained
> delusions of grandeur. (114)

Instead of obsessing over our sophisticated technologies, the Pope urges us to step back and begin reflecting on our values and our goals. He summarises his core point, 'We fail to see the deepest roots of our present failures which have to do with the direction, goals, meaning and social implications of technological and economic growth' (109).

It's not surprising then that the Pope's vision of purposeful political action is shaped by the power of local agency to effect change. While he is very critical of the ways in which politics at national or international level has been captured by the vested interests of capital, he praises the potential of more grass-roots political actions. 'While the existing world order proves powerless to assume its responsibilities, local individuals and groups can make a real difference,' he writes. He mentions cooperatives that 'ensure local self-sufficiency and even the sale of surplus energy' (179). He praises consumer movements that 'prove successful in changing the way businesses operate, forcing them to consider their environmental footprint and their patterns of production' (206). And 'the ecological movement has made significant advances, thanks also to the efforts of many organisations of civil society' (166). Overall then, the Pope's view of politics is very much a bottom-up one: 'Society, through non-governmental organisations and intermediate groups, must put pressure on governments to develop more rigorous regulations, procedures and controls. Unless citizens control political power – national, regional and municipal – it will not be possible to control damage to the environment' (179).

What impact might this have on the formal political system? Pope Francis does no more than give some hints in this regard, but they are important. He writes that 'we are always more effective when we generate processes rather than holding on to positions of power. True statecraft is manifest when, in difficult times, we uphold high principles and think of the long-term common good. Political powers do not find it easy to assume this duty in the work of nation-building' (178). The term 'statecraft' is an interesting one in that it implies that political leadership is a craft, to be exercised over the long-term and with care, at the service of nation-building. The term in the Spanish version is *grandeza política*, somewhat less specific than the English term 'statecraft'; while the term translated as 'nation-building' is *proyecto de nación*, a richer and more creative term. This is a demanding view of politics, one the Pope is all too well aware is rarely exercised in today's world. Subsequent paragraphs give us some more details of what such a view of politics entails. He writes, 'A healthy politics is sorely needed, capable of reforming and coordinating institutions, promoting best practices and overcoming undue pressure and bureaucratic inertia' (181). In a number of places, Pope Francis calls for honesty, transparency and open debate 'so that particular interests or ideologies will not prejudice the common good' (188).

It is very easy to find many examples of issues on which open debate is severely curtailed by the lobbying and power of vested interests. In the Irish situation, for example, the power of dairy agribusiness is preventing a serious debate about what forms of agriculture are needed to ensure Ireland meets its targets to reduce greenhouse gas emissions. The Pope's words, therefore, are more than pious aspirations; they have radical implications for the exercise of political power. He writes that 'what is needed is a politics which is farsighted and capable of a new, integral and interdisciplinary approach to handling the different aspects of the crisis' (197). This seems to call for a radical overhaul of our political institutions so that important issues can be addressed in a genuinely coordinated way rather than in the fragmented way that too often characterises our institutions of government. Finally, the Pope recognises that in the twenty-first century our systems of governance inherited from the past remain largely national while economic and financial power has moved to transnational levels. In this context, he returns to a topic championed by Catholic social teaching since the time of Pope John XXIII, namely 'a true world political authority' (175). As subsequent popes have recognised, this is even more urgent in today's globalised world in which economic and financial power have migrated beyond the effective reach of the nation state.

Civic and Political Love

Perhaps the richest reflection of all on politics in this encyclical comes towards the end. A section in the final chapter is entitled 'Civic and Political Love' and in this Pope Francis affirms, 'Love, overflowing with small gestures of mutual care, is also civic and political, and it makes itself felt in every action that seeks to build a better world' (231). Later, in the same paragraph, he links this to social love and to spirituality when he writes that:

> along with the importance of little everyday gestures, social love moves us to devise larger strategies to halt environmental degradation and to encourage a 'culture of care' which permeates all of society. When we feel that God is calling us to intervene with others in these social dynamics, we should realise that this too is part of our spirituality, which is an exercise of charity and, as such, matures and sanctifies us.

There has rarely been a more beautiful and profound expression of the call to political and social action to build a better world. This, then, invokes the sense of personal responsibility that must lie at the heart of all political and social action, mentioned as 'a sense of social responsibility' (206) and as 'personal qualities of self-control and willingness to learn from one another' (214).

Finally, the call to personal responsibility and commitment is directed by Pope Francis, not just to civil society but to politicians themselves. In *Evangelii Gaudium* he writes, 'I ask God to give us more politicians capable of sincere and effective dialogue aimed at healing the deepest roots – and not simply the appearances – of the evils in our world! Politics, though often denigrated, remains a lofty vocation and one of the highest forms of charity, inasmuch as it seeks the common good.' He begs the Lord:

> to grant us more politicians who are genuinely disturbed by the state of society, the people, the lives of the poor! It is vital that government leaders and financial leaders take heed and broaden their horizons, working to ensure that all citizens have dignified work, education and healthcare. Why not turn to God and ask him to inspire their plans? (205)

The understanding and importance of politics that finds expression in *Laudato Si'*, therefore, addresses substantially the 'reconciliation between ethics, economics, ecology and cultural diversity' called for by President Higgins in Istanbul. In an age when politics is widely and routinely denigrated and appears incapable of providing the leadership and action needed to address the most grave of crises faced by humanity, the significance of these reflections on politics cannot be overstated. They lay out an agenda for political leadership without which the transition to a low-carbon society will be impossible.

Walking the Road from Paris

JOHN SWEENEY

Introduction

Achieving a unanimous agreement at COP21 in Paris in December 2015 involving one hundred and ninety five countries with widely varying national agendas represented a historic triumph for diplomacy and a recognition that the seriousness of climate change was at last acknowledged across the world stage. Memories of the abortive Copenhagen Conference in 2009 had haunted the preparations for the conference and a second failure on this scale was unthinkable. Thus, a detailed choreography leading up to COP21 involving the United Nations, the Intergovernmental Panel on Climate Change, the Vatican, and the tireless efforts of the French diplomatic system was undertaken. This paid off and, despite some last-minute hitches, the first legally binding global agreement on climate change – requiring action by both the developing and developed countries – was adopted and will enter into force in 2020. On 4 November 2016, the agreement became a binding treaty following its ratification by fifty-five countries accounting for at least 55 per cent of global emissions. The rapidity with which this occurred was largely unprecedented in the history of international agreements. Notwithstanding the success story so far, and aside from recent setbacks due to the actions of the US administration, the agreement has its flaws. The omission of shipping and aviation emissions (in total equivalent to the national emissions of the UK and Germany combined), the vagueness regarding timetables and emission reductions, the lip service paid to human rights and climate justice, and the general lack of urgency pervading the actions to be taken before and after 2020, were all disappointing. But overall a framework has been created in which five-yearly reviews of national pledges promise a progressively increasing effort on the part of both the developed and the developing world to plan for a post-carbon world.

Delegates, however, were motivated primarily by national self-interest. The brief they had been tasked with was generally to ensure that their country's particular circumstances were not disadvantaged by whatever agreement emerged. Such considerations, of course, are the reason it has taken twenty-one years to achieve any global agreement to tackle climate change. These have deep historical roots. The problems of regulating the international 'commons' can be traced back to 1648 and the Treaty of Westphalia, which ended the Thirty Years' War in Europe. From then on, the sovereign state became the entity to replace local and regional power groups. Ultimately, nation states became the relevant bodies in international law and the global order. But placing national before global good remains the major obstacle to successful implementation of the Paris Agreement in an increasingly globalised world. This chapter outlines the two pillars on which progress must be built to overcome this obstacle: scientific and ethical.

Science Must Inform National Policy

The Intergovernmental Panel on Climate Change

The Fifth Assessment Report of the Intergovernmental Panel on Climate Change (AR5) provided a substantial evidence base on which any international policy response should be anchored. AR5 produced greater certainty about several aspects of climate change based on more comprehensive observations, more sophisticated modelling and better understanding of the complexities of the earth-atmosphere system. The headline statement that 'it is at least 95 per cent likely that human activities – chiefly the burning of fossil fuels – are the main cause of warming since the 1950s' was accompanied by a number of key findings as follows:

- Global temperatures have increased by 0.85°C over the period 1880–2012 and about 0.5°C over the period 1979–2010. Substantial decadal and interannual variability has accompanied this clear warming trend due to natural variability in the climate system.

- The warming has been greater over land than over the ocean and greater in mid-to-high latitude parts of the globe. Heatwaves have increased in frequency. Each of the last three decades has been warmer than all preceding decades since 1850. The thirty-year period from 1981–2010 was the warmest of the last eight hundred years.

- Global precipitation has not changed significantly over the course of the twentieth century though an increasing precipitation trend exists in middle and high latitudes of the northern hemisphere, especially since the 1950s. Intense rainfall events have increased in frequency significantly in a majority of regions, especially Europe and North America.

- Tropical Atlantic storms have increased in intensity, though trends in other areas are not clear.

- Greenland is melting much more quickly in recent years with average losses per year six times higher than in the early 1990s. Arctic sea ice cover has decreased by 4 per cent per decade since 1979, with mean winter sea ice thickness having halved. The Antarctic ice sheet is now losing mass five times faster than in the early 1990s.
- Sea level rise has accelerated from 1.7 mm per year over the twentieth century to 3.2 mm per year over the past two decades.

In the event that global greenhouse gas emissions continue to increase along the present trajectory, a further rise in temperature of 0.5°C is likely over the next twenty years, and over the next eighty-five years only a fifty-fifty chance of avoiding a 4°C rise over pre-industrial levels would exist. For most parts of the world, the frequency of the once-in-twenty-year maximum temperature will double. Indeed, for many regions it will become ten to twenty times more frequent with a high likelihood that more frequent and longer duration heatwaves will occur. Should global greenhouse gas emissions continue on their present trend, the high latitudes and the equatorial Pacific are expected to experience an increase in annual mean precipitation while in many mid-latitude and subtropical dry regions, mean precipitation will likely decrease. Extreme precipitation events over most of the mid-latitude land masses and over wet tropical regions will very likely become more intense and more frequent.

Recent Scientific Advances

Since the publication of AR5, the science has advanced. Contrarians often cherry-picked the year 1998 as the start of a supposed trend showing a pause or hiatus in warming; however, this argument has now been demonstrated as fallacious.[1] It is now clear that an underestimation of volcanic activity[2] and a preponderance of cool La Niña events combined to hide the warming trend from 1998–2013, as did the movement of atmospheric heat energy into the deep ocean.[3] Choosing to start a trend analysis arbitrarily from the record warm year of 1998 is dubious statistically, and, moreover, it is now clear that there was no real hiatus in global warming. There was no significant change in the warming rate in the immediate pre- and post-1998 periods.[4] The warmest year in the instrumental record was 2016, as were 2015 and 2014 previously. Of course, this was partly as a consequence of the record El Niño event in the Pacific, and it should not be assumed that such a succession of record warm years will continue once La Niña returns. Nonetheless, 2017 is likely to be among the top five warmest years on record. The renewed warmth of recent years means that the earth's surface temperature has increased by 1.1°C since the late nineteenth century, halfway to the 2°C threshold at which dangerous climate change is expected and also halfway to the limitation agreed at Paris. It means sixteen of the seventeen warmest years on record have occurred since 2000.

For countries on the fringes of a warming ocean, the immediate consequences come in terms of increased storms and rain. The winter of 2013/14 was the stormiest in the area of Britain and Ireland since records began more than one hundred and forty years ago.[5] When the warmed air mass is pulled from tropical marine locations, an atmospheric river – a narrow corridor of concentrated atmospheric moisture – can produce exceptional rainfall events far removed from the source. This was instrumental in producing the serious flood event in Ireland and north-west England in 2009 and again in 2015/16. On 5 December 2015, 344.1 mm of rain was recorded in Cumbria, a new UK daily rainfall record. Most of Ireland experienced its wettest winter on record in 2015/16, partly as a result of such a phenomenon. Again, it should be emphasised that while such extreme events are expected to increase in frequency as global climate changes, individual seasons and years will show contrary trends on occasion as natural controls such as atmospheric blocking and oceanic circulations interact with the global trend. Cherry-picking of short-term trends should not be used either to undermine the overall global trend to warming nor to exaggerate its rate of change.

Contrarian arguments have also centred on climate sensitivity, which is normally considered to be the temperature change associated with a doubling of greenhouse gas concentration. In AR5, this was widened from that of AR4 to encompass a range from 1.5–4.5°C. While some interpreted this as indicating increased uncertainty in climate models, it is now clear that this was an artefact of the IPCC process, which lists, but does not query, the range of research outputs in an area. In fact, more recent work has raised questions about the assumptions underlying the lower estimates involved and has reaffirmed that the best estimate for a world with doubled greenhouse gas loading is, in fact, 3°C.[6] In mid-2017, global CO_2 concentrations exceeded 408 ppm compared with pre-industrial levels of 278 ppm. When other greenhouse gases are taken into account, the current figure for CO_2 equivalent concentration is closer to 480 ppm.

There is also growing concern that the role of methane is not adequately represented in calculations of CO_2 equivalent emissions. This is usually done through deriving the Global Warming Potential (GWP), a measure of the amount of heat trapped in the atmosphere by a particular mass of a gas compared to a similar mass of carbon dioxide. In calculations of the GWP of a basket of greenhouse gases, methane has been weighted as twenty-five times more potent than CO_2. This is the figure used in current emission calculations in international agreements and is based on the recommendations of the IPCC Fourth Assessment Report (AR4). However, AR5 recommended a figure of thirty-four and this is likely to be the recommended figure for future GWP calculations. In addition, there is a robust scientific discussion as to the timescale to be used for GWP calculations, currently set at a hundred years, reflecting CO_2's slow turnover time in the atmosphere. Methane, however, has a shorter atmospheric lifetime of approximately twelve years and AR5, therefore, states that 'there is no scientific argument for selecting one hundred years'. In July 2014, a group of prominent scientists wrote to President Obama urging the US to also employ a twenty-year horizon for methane calculations in GWP. In this time frame the weighting for methane recommended by AR5 is eighty-six. Such a revision would have major consequences for large methane emitters, such as Ireland. But the scientific message is clear: methane's contribution to overall warming is probably seriously underestimated. It also follows that targeting methane emission reductions offers good potential for slowing warming in the short and medium term.

Scientific literature since AR5 shows increasing concern in the area of sea level rise. Estimates of sea level rise in AR4 were widely considered to be too conservative, and were perhaps the most controversial aspect of that report. These ranged from 0.18 m to 0.59 m for the end of the current century compared with the end of the last one. For AR5 these values were increased to 0.28–0.98 m. However, the lower end of these estimates would require radical greenhouse gas emission reductions starting in a few years and global emissions becoming negative after six decades. Uncertainties as to how the Greenland and Antarctic ice sheets will behave are also part of what may still be considered to be conservative projections. Since AR5, concerns have emerged that ice shelves in Antarctica could disintegrate more quickly, pulling more land-based ice into the ocean. A potential contribution of over 1 m by 2100 from Antarctica alone has been suggested[7] and as further knowledge of the response of the polar zones to warming emerges, the risk is clearly on the increase. Anthropogenic carbon emissions up to 2000 have already committed the planet to 1.7 m of sea level rise. A similar emission quantity post 2000 would commit the planet to a further 9 m rise as the Antarctic and Greenland ice caps melt out, though this would take several centuries to be realised.[8]

It is clear that hard choices will have to be made to tackle climate change. These must be based on the best available scientific information as to causes, consequences and possible mitigation actions. The first step is to recognise the scale of the problem and accept that the scientific message is unambiguous. Urgent action to tackle an emergent planetary emergency is required. While it may be more comfortable for some to make excuses for inaction and downplay the seriousness of the global predicament involved, procrastination is not an option. The science must inform the imminent policy choices to be made.

Ethical Considerations Must Inform Policy

The Polluter Pays/Intergenerational Equity

Traditionally the atmosphere has been looked upon as a free resource, with unregulated access. The problems of managing such resources were most famously articulated by Hardin (1968) in his classic essay 'The Tragedy of the Commons'.[9] This highlighted the imperative of individuals to act in their own self-interest irrespective of the contribution it was making to the destruction of the resource as a whole. Climate change epitomises this problem, with individuals and nations acting in their own self-interest, irrespective of the global common good. To tackle such a problem, intervention in the form of regulation or licensing is the only workable option. This ultimately leads to the 'polluter pays' principle, whereby the utilisation cost of access to the atmosphere must be paid for proportionately by those who pollute it. Damage costs should not be borne by society at large. For climate change, however, there is another complication due to the time delay between emissions and impacts. The cost of delayed or ineffective action on climate change will accrue not just to today's inhabitants of the planet, but to their children and their descendants. The principle of intergenerational equity then comes into play, and indeed has already formed the basis for legal action against greenhouse gas polluters in some jurisdictions. In April 2016 a federal court in Eugene, Oregon ruled in favour of twenty-one young plaintiffs across the USA who sued the federal government for violating their constitutional rights to life, liberty and property as a result of government action and inaction resulting in 'carbon pollution of the atmosphere'.[10]

Common But Differentiated Responsibility

The principle most often quoted in international climate negotiations is the principle of common but differentiated responsibility. This formed the basis of the United Nations Framework Convention on Climate Change which entered into force on 21 March 1994. This has two basic aspects. Firstly, it ascribes a common responsibility to each country to protect the integrity of the environment at national and global levels. Secondly, it recognises the need to take into consideration the particular circumstances of each country, particularly in terms of its contribution to the problem over time and its capability of contributing to its resolution. Thus, for example, while a country such as Ireland emits more greenhouse gases in a given year than the four hundred million poorest people on the planet, and while both Ireland and the four hundred million poorest people have a common responsibility to protect and preserve their common resource – the atmosphere – the respective efforts involved should obviously be very different. Developed countries bear a greater responsibility historically for creating the problem and also a greater capacity to mitigate and adapt to climate change. This is the main plank underpinning international agreements such as Paris and also the financial transfers to foster a sustainable development trajectory for developing countries (e.g. the Green Climate Fund).

Integral Ecology

Although the term 'wicked problem' was originally used to describe problems associated with social policy, the expression has frequently been seen as applicable to climate change.[11] Essentially, this is a problem that can only be solved if a sufficiently large portion of the population radically change their mindsets and behaviour, and that cannot be tackled piecemeal, but requires a holistic perspective. Climate change qualifies as a wicked problem. The need for a holistic perspective is perhaps the single most important reason that progress in tackling climate change has been so ponderously slow. From a governance perspective, almost every department would see a role for itself in addressing the problem from its particular point of view. Administrative silos are also accompanied by disciplinary silos, whereby the multifaceted dimensions of the problem are not properly appreciated, leading to a selective response framed in a narrow political or economic perspective. Often this is heavily influenced by powerful groups with vested interests.

One of the most influential statements on the need to develop an integrated approach to climate change has come from the papal encyclical *Laudato Si'*. Founded on a strong and well-articulated exposition of the science, this encyclical explores the interconnections between climate change and the human condition from an ethical, moral and theological perspective. Theologically, the encyclical finally dispels the myth of anthropocentrism, the notion that the human species has an inalienable right to 'go forth and subdue the earth'. Rather than this literal interpretation of the Book of Genesis, which has pervaded both religious and political creeds for too long, an ethic of care for all of nature's creatures is stressed. All life has value, irrespective of its utility to humans and humans have no rights to reduce this richness and diversity to satisfy short-term irresponsible needs. In particular, the importance of 'integral ecology' is emphasised. It is argued that interconnected problems, such as climate change, poverty and economic development, demand an integrated strategy that includes the protection of nature and of the rights of all occupants of our common home. Only then can those difficult-to-quantify components of the environment under threat, such as biodiversity, be incorporated on the basis of their intrinsic worth and not seen solely as exploitable resources. Although such a holistic approach would appear to be an essential pillar for climate negotiations, the segmentation of responsibilities among negotiators makes it difficult to implement in practice. Few individuals have the necessary perspective to see beyond their silo and this has bedevilled tackling climate change at both national and international levels.

Although a fuller discussion of *Laudato Si'* occurs elsewhere in this text, and it has been extensively reviewed by Sean McDonagh, two further aspects on integral ecology are worth discussing.[12] The first is the utility it offers to link 'ecological debt' to financial debt. Developed countries have historically exploited the natural environment to fuel their development, especially the fossil energy sources. They now wish to constrain developing countries from doing likewise due to the climate consequences this would bring. An ecological debt exists on the part of the developed countries; implicit recognition of which comes in the form of financial transfers to the developing countries. This relationship links human and natural rights to more practical issues of compensation, legal and financial redress and, ultimately, how the developed world should interact with the developing world to ensure a global accord on climate.

Secondly, *Laudato Si'* emphasises the need to move away from a solely economics-based view of the natural world and reminds us that climate change is essentially a moral and ethical problem. This is a challenging paradigm shift for decision makers steeped in conventional cost-benefit analysis concepts. Yet political leaders who shy away from making the hard decisions necessary to address climate change issues should, the encyclical emphasises, be held to account by the communities they represent. Interestingly, a number of prominent Catholic groups filed an *amicus curiae* (friend of the court) brief in support of the legal action in Oregon.[13] Considerations of intergenerational equity and of what is termed 'the common good' are seen as essential building blocks to grow human solidarity towards the protection of the natural world.

Informed by the science, an ethical framework for guiding policy to tackle climate change is essential. Without this, short-term vested interests shape policy and coming generations are bequeathed a damaged planet with limited options for sustainability. Ethics must inform policy to confer responsibility for implementing the required changes to avoid this scenario.

The Remaining Carbon Budget: The Elephant in the Room

Neither science nor ethical arguments were prominent in the Paris negotiations, especially as they related to the equity considerations which might be involved in allocating the remaining capacity of the earth-atmosphere system to absorb greenhouse gases without causing dangerous climate change. One of the most startling findings of AR5 was the strong linear correlation between cumulative greenhouse emissions and global temperature change. The long residence time for CO_2 in the atmosphere means that we are today experiencing the continued warming effect of gas emitted a century ago. The warming of just under 1°C that has occurred over the past century corresponds to a cumulative emission of approximately 2,000 GtCO2. This latest carbon budget relationship shows that total future CO_2 emissions cannot exceed 1200 GtCO2 for a likely (66 per cent) chance of keeping average global warming under 2°C since pre-industrial times (Figure 1). Nations have agreed that going beyond this limit risks 'dangerous' climate change and this was the chief motivation for the Paris Agreement. At the current rate of CO_2 emissions, this 1200 GtCO2 'quota' will be used up in around thirty years – or one generation. Current global emissions will consume the remaining carbon budget to avoid 1.5°C warming probably within a decade or two. The window of opportunity is closing rapidly.

What Next?

The headline statement of AR5 was that 'it is at least 95 per cent likely that human activities – chiefly the burning of fossil fuels – are the main cause of warming since the 1950s'. This degree of scientific certainty and myriad international pressures have not, however, produced adequate national responses. The pledges made by countries in Paris through their Intended Nationally Determined Contributions (INDCs) would, if fully realised, still condemn the world to 2.7°C warming within the next eighty-five years.[14] Should little or no action occur in key countries before the 2020 commencement date, the pathway to avoid the 2°C threshold will become very difficult. Indeed, several countries include plans for as yet untested technologies such as carbon capture and storage in their INDCs. It is clear that a failure to overcome national self-interest remains, as does a failure to produce a political response beyond the short-term exigencies of the political cycle in many countries. Turning the Paris vision of a low carbon future into reality requires concerted international action and pressure on decision makers from their electorate below and their supranational overseers above.

From above, resolute leadership is required. An encouraging start on this was demonstrated by the two largest polluters, the US and China, who reached a bilateral agreement in advance of the Paris conference. The US undertook to reduce its greenhouse gas emissions by 26–28 per cent on 2005 levels by 2020 and 83 per cent by 2050. China has undertaken to peak its emissions by 2030 or earlier and increase its share of non-fossil fuels in primary energy consumption to 20 per cent by the same date. While both countries' commitments are modest in terms of what is needed, the fact that together the two countries account for over half of global emissions made this a significant first step.

The announcement by President Donald Trump in June 2017 that the US was withdrawing from the Paris Agreement and the subsequent dismantling of national efforts to tackle climate change undermines the bilateral accord with China and has damaged the international reputation of the US on the global stage. The agreement was carefully crafted to take account of US political sensitivities and withdrawal is not legally possible until November 2020; however, no sanctions for non-compliance with emission targets exist. While the US may technically remain an adherent to the treaty, and subject to reporting requirements, any leadership functions and influence it formerly had within the UNFCCC will now pass to other nations, particularly China, and to a lesser extent the European Union. From an economic perspective, many countries will now likely consider that a level playing field no longer exists with the US and climate change issues are likely to emerge in trade negotiations with what the former United Nations' envoy on climate change Mary Robinson has described as a 'rogue state'.

The European Union has traditionally been in a leadership role in international agreements to combat climate change, though it was marginalised in the years following the ill-fated Copenhagen Conference of 2009. Nonetheless, a long-term cost-effective road map for reducing greenhouse gas emissions by 80–95 per cent on 1990 levels was published by the EU Commission in 2011. This envisaged a reduction of 20 per cent in emissions by 2020, 40 per cent by 2030, 60 per cent by 2040 and 80–95 per cent by 2050. The first of these targets was agreed by the European Council and the European Parliament and obliges member states to contribute differentially according to their ability, principally determined by their gross domestic product (GDP) per capita. Ireland, with one of the highest GDPs per capita is obliged to meet a 20 per cent target, and is currently on track to fail this. This is principally as a result of what is deemed to be an overarching priority to expand agriculture and an inability to control transport emissions. The passage of the Climate and Low Carbon Development Bill in late 2015 contains no short- or long-term targets or sanctions and a general lack of commitment to meeting national obligations is evident. Subsidies of €125 million per annum are still provided by the taxpayer to support peat-burning power stations, and adaptation plans, other than flood protection, are poorly integrated into sectoral policies. Returning to the EU scale, negotiations for the 2030 period foresee the 40 per cent reduction required being met by a 43 per cent reduction in those (mainly industrial) sources regulated by the Emissions Trading System and a 30 per cent reduction (on 2005 levels) coming from the remaining sectors (agriculture, transport, buildings, waste). Special case pleading, based on national self-interest, has featured strongly in these negotiations, particularly from Ireland. A national Irish obligation of a further 10 per cent reduction from the 2020 figure by 2030 has been diluted by concessions amounting to potentially 9.6 per cent. While aspects of the concessions proposed for Ireland are being opposed by other member states and the EU Parliament, strong lobbying to permit increasing Irish emissions to occur without fines being levied is evident. Overcoming narrow national self-interest by a strong European leadership position based on a 'fair share' mitigation pathway (Figure 2) would seem to be the only way forward, and this, as yet, is not convincingly evident.

From below, sensitisation of the general public to the issues surrounding climate change is a slow process, though increasingly catalysed by extreme events such as flooding. Despite the misinformation provided by some elements of the tabloid media, there is some evidence, at least in the UK, that awareness of the scientific consensus on climate change is growing.[15] Increased activity by civil society also enhances electoral pressures on policymakers as a better educated and more vociferous public convey their concerns, likely even through legal challenges. But perhaps the fastest growing manifestation of pressure from below is coming from the rapid growth of the divestment movement. Individuals and organisations asking for their money to be moved out of oil, coal and gas companies is a relatively recent but increasingly influential process. Led by the universities and religious institutions, the movement has quickly embraced pension funds, local authorities and charitable foundations. Universities such as Stanford (USA), Glasgow (UK) and Maynooth (Ireland) have divested, as have influential funds such as the Rockefeller Brothers Fund (heirs to the founder of Standard Oil). While new investors take up such stock, albeit frequently at a lower share price, the reality of the need to leave 80 per cent of known fossil fuel reserves in the ground to avoid dangerous climate change creates an increasingly obvious investment risk. The risk of unburnable reserves becoming stranded assets increases as the divestment movement grows. By the end of 2016, one estimate was that the value of assets represented by institutions and individuals committing to some sort of divestment from fossil fuel companies had reached $5 trillion.[16] The momentum of the divestment movement as part of a wider public sensitisation to climate change issues can, therefore, no longer be ignored by policymakers.

Conclusions

Walking the road from Paris, there will be many twists and turns. Following the signposts provided by authoritative scientific opinion provides the safest way. Attempts to subvert this by those with an alternative agenda should be avoided, using ethical principles to ensure no one is left behind and no one is bullied into going backwards. Leadership and vision are the essential ingredients for a safe arrival in a decarbonised world. Where these are lacking or weak, people must take charge of their own futures for the sake of their children and for the sake of all inhabitants of what *Laudato Si'* refers to as our common home.

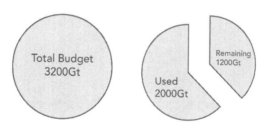

Figure 1: Total budget to have a 2:1 chance of avoiding 2°C warming. Remaining budget is equivalent to approximately thirty years at current rates of emisson.[17]

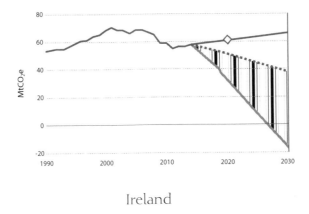

Ireland

Figure 2: The Stockholm Climate Equity Reference Calculator output for Ireland. The main line shows the 'fair share' mitigation pathway for a 2°C warming limit based on the remaining carbon budget allocation for Ireland. After the middle of the 2020s the line crosses the zero axis, indicating Ireland will have used up its fair share. The top line indicates the present trajectory based on business as usual in Ireland. The dashed line shows the trajectory necessary to conform with the global objectives. The gap between the top and bottom lines indicates Ireland's climate justice debt to the developing world.[18]

Endnotes

1.   T. Karl et al., 'Possible artifacts of data biases in the recent global surface warming hiatus', *Science*, 2015, 348:6242, pp. 1469–72.

2.   D. Santer et al., 'Observed multivariable signals of late 20th and early 21st century volcanic activity', *Geophysical Research Letters*, 2015, 42:2, pp. 500–9.

3.   X. Chen and K. Tung, 'Varying planetary heat sink led to global-warming slowdown and acceleration', *Science*, 2014, 345:6199, pp. 897–903.

4.   N. Cahill, S. Rahmstorf and A. Parnell, 'Change points of global temperature', *Environmental Research Letters*, 2015, 10:8, pp. 1–6.

5.   T. Matthews, C. Murphy, R.L. Wilby and S. Harrigan, 'A cyclone climatology of the British-Irish Isles 1871–2012', *International Journal of Climatology*, 2016, 36:3, pp. 1299–1312.

6. K. Marvel, G.A. Schmidt, R.L. Miller and L.S. Nazarenko, 'Implications for climate sensitivity from the response to individual forcings', *Nature Climate Change*, 2015, 6:4, pp. 386–89.

7. R.M. DeConto and D. Pollard, 'Contribution of Antarctica to past and future sea-level rise', *Nature*, 2016, 531:7596, pp. 591–7.

8. P.U. Clark, J.D. Shakun, S.A. Marcott, A.C. Mix, M. Eby, S. Kulp, A. Levermann, G.A. Milne, P.L. Pfister, B.D. Santer, D.P. Schrag, S. Solomon, T. Stocker, B.H. Strauss, A.J. Weaver, R. Winkelmann, D. Archer, E. Bard, A. Goldner, K. Lambeck, R.T. Pierrehumbert and G. Plattner, 'Consequences of twenty-first-century policy for multi-millennial climate and sea-level change', *Nature Climate Change*, 2016, 6:4, pp. 360–9.

9. G. Hardin, 'The Tragedy of the Commons', *Science*, 1968, 162:3859, pp. 1243–8.

10. Federal Climate Change Lawsuit, 2016, www.ourchildrenstrust.org/us/federal-lawsuit. Accessed 14 May 2016.

11. H. Rittel and M. Webber, 'Dilemmas in a General Theory of Planning', *Policy Sciences*, 1973, 4, pp. 155–69.

12. Sean McDonagh, *On Care for Our Common Home, Laudato Si'*, New York: Orbis Books, 2016.

13. Federal Climate Change Lawsuit, 2016.

14. International Energy Agency, *Energy and Climate Change*, Paris: OECD/IEA, 2015.

15. ComRes, 'ECIU Survey on Energy and Climate Change', 2015, www.comres.co.uk/polls/eciu-survey-on-energy-and-climate-change. Accessed 14 May 2016.

16. Arabella Advisors, *Measuring the Growth of the Global Fossil Fuel Divestment and Clean Energy Investment Movement*, Washington DC: Arabella Advisors, 2015.

17. P. Friedlingstein, R.M. Andrew, J. Rogelj, G.P. Peters, J.G. Canadell, R. Knutti, G. Luderer, M.R. Raupach, M. Schaeffer, D.P. van Vuuren and C. Le Quéré, 'Persistent growth of CO_2 emissions and implications for reaching climate target', *Nature Geoscience*, 2014, 7:10, pp. 709–15.

18. Stockholm Environment Institute, climateequityreference.org.

From Vatican II to *Laudato Si'*

DONAL DORR

Historians say that it takes an ecumenical council at least fifty years to take full effect. This is undoubtedly true of Vatican II, which ended fifty years ago. One of its most significant achievements was to take a major step in rescuing us from the dualistic theology and spirituality in which Christians had been trapped for centuries. This enabled us to be guided by the Holy Spirit in 'reading the signs of the times'. It opened up a door for four major unforeseen developments in spirituality and theology. The first three of these enormously important developments emerged just a few years after the council; the fourth was much slower to emerge and its quite radical nature and significance is only now beginning to be accepted.

Humanistic Psychology

In the Western world, shortly after the council ended in 1965, we became aware of the significance for spirituality and theology of the humanistic psychology that was beginning to flourish at that time. We now take it for granted that in terms of spiritual direction and religious education there is a deep connection between personal development and spirituality. But we have only to look at any of the pre-Vatican II manuals of what was called 'ascetical theology' (for instance, *The Spiritual Life* by A. Tanqueray) to be reminded of how the writers of these manuals took little or no account of developments in human psychology. Most probably they chose to ignore these developments, believing that spiritual advancement took place in a realm that was largely independent of, and 'higher' than, psychological healing and development. It is important to note that it was not Vatican II that *caused* us to now take for granted a seamless connection between personal development, on the one hand, and spirituality, spiritual direction and religious education on the other hand. The council simply removed the blindfold that had prevented us from seeing the significance of the new developments taking place in the so-called 'secular world'. We were then able to transform our spirituality by taking full account of Jungian and humanist psychology, as well as the Western appropriation of the Eastern wisdom associated with the Enneagram.

Feminist Theology and Spirituality

At its best, Vatican II brought us liberation from dualistic thinking – the soul in contrast to the body, the spiritual in contrast to the worldly or temporal, the future in contrast to the present, the clergy in contrast to the laity. This opened the door for women and men who were not part of the clerical establishment to study theology, to develop spirituality, and to become spiritual directors and teachers of theology. There was now space for theologians – particularly the new women theologians – to take account of the feminist thought which began to flourish around this time in secular society. They could 'see in the women's movement the working of the Spirit', as Pope Francis acknowledged fifty years later in his apostolic exhortation, *Amoris Laetitia* (54). The result has been an enormous enrichment in our understanding of the scriptures, in our theology and our spirituality – and a challenge to the previous mainstream understanding of scripture, theology and spirituality that is quite radical.

Liberation Theology and Spirituality

Parallel to these two developments of spirituality and theology in the Western world there was the emergence of liberation theology, first in Latin America and then in Asia, Africa, and among minority groups in the Western world. Like feminist theology, this liberationist approach has posed a radical challenge to mainstream theology and brought a wonderful enrichment to our understanding of the message of the Bible. Once again, the primary sources of the new insights did not come from within the older theology but from outside. In this case they came from two sources: from dialogue with very poor people whose faith came to be appreciated as a crucial channel of revelation; and from the work of some scholars who, influenced by a more recent humanistic version of Marxism, were reading the Bible with new eyes, and developing a radical critique of the dominant economic, political and educational theory and practice of the time. One striking example is the enormous influence on liberation theology and spirituality of the work of the Brazilian educationalist and campaigner Paulo Freire. There may be many today who still remain somewhat suspicious of liberation theology and spirituality. However, Pope Francis offers a rejoinder to this, as is clear from the text of the two quite radical addresses that he gave to social and political activists in Rome in October 2014 and in Bolivia in July 2015.[1]

Those who have moved from an older spirituality to one which embraces one, two or all three of the above new approaches may recall how this involved a change of mentality and mindset, and also of perspective and outlook, and how it involved noticing things which previously they would have overlooked. All this led them to *feel* differently about situations. This, in turn, led on to a rather different set of priorities about how they understood situations and what actions they took. This whole process can be described as a kind of *conversion*. In some cases, this conversion may have been relatively easy and minor; for others, it was rather more difficult and perhaps more gradual, marked by some resistance on their part – particularly if the change only came about as a result of being challenged painfully by somebody whose views they respected.

Ecological Theology and Spirituality

The three major developments that I have mentioned offer us such rich opportunities for developing our spirituality that we may not pay sufficient attention to a hugely important breakthrough in spirituality that has emerged more slowly and is only now beginning to transform our whole understanding of our Christian faith. Like the other developments mentioned above, this would not have been possible if Vatican II had not rescued us from dualistic and escapist conceptions of faith. But, again like the other developments, it is not something that emerged from within mainstream theology and spirituality. Rather its real source is the advances which have taken place in the secular sciences of biology, chemistry, physics and geology. Above all, it comes from our understanding of the process of evolution. To comprehend the full implications of this new understanding calls for a *conversion* of mentality, perspective, feelings and actions. This is the 'ecological conversion' which Pope Francis calls for in his wonderful encyclical, *Laudato Si'* (cf. 217–21).

The central theme which runs right throughout Pope Francis' encyclical is 'ecological conversion'. Francis gives quite a detailed account of various dimensions of this conversion – economic, political, social, cultural, and religious.[2] Here, I shall focus on just one aspect of the religious dimension, leaving to other contributors an account of the other aspects of an ecological conversion as outlined by Pope Francis in his encyclical.

The Many Elements in Ecological Conversion

The first and most essential element in an ecological conversion is coming to an effective awareness and acceptance that everything in our world is connected. This is a point which Pope Francis emphasises strongly and repeatedly in *Laudato Si'* (cf. 16, 42, 70, 91, 117, 138, 220, 240). We humans are an integral part of creation, linked to every other creature and every object in our universe. More specifically, Francis describes this interconnection of things as a *network*, referring to 'the mysterious network of relations between things' (20); 'the complex network of ecosystems' (134); and pointing out that 'living species are part of a network which we will never fully explore and understand' (138).

Ecologists call this network the 'web of life', which includes animals, plants and everything which can be understood to be alive. They also speak of 'the web of the cosmos', which includes the non-living parts of our universe, ranging from the most distant galaxies to the most microscopic elements. This is a good image of the extent to which each element in our world is linked to everything else, because whenever anything touches any part of a spiderweb, the whole web trembles. We dare not interfere with any aspect of the world around us without being aware that our action may have unforeseen consequences. For this reason, a key part of our spirituality must include a sense of being an integral part of an interconnected universe. As Francis says, we need to have 'a loving awareness that we are not disconnected from the rest of creatures, but joined in a splendid universal communion' (220).

This leads on to the second key point which is to know *why* everything is connected. It is because everything in our universe has its origin in the Big Bang which took place 13,750,000 years ago. That incredible explosion of energy gave rise, after a billion years, to the formation of a hundred million galaxies. The galaxy in which our world exists is called the Milky Way; it contains billions of stars. In our galaxy, about 4,600,000 years after the initial Big Bang, exploding stars dissolved into dust. Some of this dust, in turn, coalesced into other stars, one of which is our own sun. Some of the remaining cosmic dust formed the planets, including planet earth. In this world, which is our home, there emerged, over billions of years, the seas, the land, and the air. Much later came the water-creatures, the plants, the animals and eventually the various branches of humanity. Every rock, tree, animal and person all have a common origin; all are composed of the same cosmic material (which some people call 'star stuff'), and all are related to each other.

Evolution and The New Story

When we ask how it is that the same cosmic material has come to take such amazingly different forms, the answer is the process of evolution. So the next aspect of an ecological conversion is to come to understand something of this process of evolution. This is what the great ecological theologian and Passionist priest Thomas Berry called the New Story of creation. If we deny or ignore the process of evolution then we are not adequately aware of our own identity. Of course, this New Story should not be seen as a replacement for the story of creation as told in the Bible. The Genesis story does not attempt to give a chronological account of creation. The key point of that story is that every aspect of our world is created by God and is good – and that when God looked at creation in its totality, 'God saw that it was very good' (Gn 1:31). What the New Story offers us is a rich insight into the nature of our universe. It gives us some sense of its great age and its astonishing size and variety. It opens up for us an awareness of the actual stages of the development of our present world and the amazingly complex emergence of the extraordinary diversity of its life forms, including ourselves. It helps to bring home to us how everything is linked to everything else in the network to which Francis refers. Finally, it invites us to appreciate the fact that what we have is by no means a static network, but one which is constantly giving rise to new changes. So we don't just look back at the developments that led to our present situation but also look forward to future developments.

It is a pity that Francis did not have more to say in the encyclical about the process of evolution, since it is evolution which explains how it is that everything is connected. When he referred to the contribution of Teilhard de Chardin (53), it would have been a good opportunity to also make at least a brief reference to the work of Thomas Berry and the concept of the New Story.[3] Perhaps Francis felt that to do so might distract from what he saw as the more urgent need to challenge those who deny or play down the reality of climate change and the fact that humans are mainly responsible for it.

Integral Ecology

Pope Francis proposes what he calls an 'integral ecology'. Pope John Paul and Pope Benedict tended to emphasise the *difference* between humans and other creatures, setting 'human ecology' over against so-called 'natural ecology'. On the other hand, Francis emphasises all that humans have in common with the rest of creation. For example, he says, 'A good part of our genetic code is shared by many living beings ... Nature cannot be regarded as something separate from ourselves or as a mere setting in which we live. We are part of nature, included in it' (138–9).

For Francis, the term 'human ecology' refers particularly to how our actions and whole way of life affects other creatures and the whole environment. Since the term 'integral ecology' is a very wide one, it can be used to include the protection of the unborn. Francis says:

> Since everything is interrelated, concern for the protection of nature is also incompatible with the justification of abortion. How can we genuinely teach the importance of concern for other vulnerable beings, however troublesome or inconvenient they may be, if we fail to protect a human embryo, even when its presence is uncomfortable and creates difficulties? (120; cf. 117)

A Contemplative Spirituality

The 'ecological spirituality' (216) put forward by Pope Francis is the fruit of an ecological conversion. It has both an active aspect and a more receptive or contemplative dimension. A very large part of his encyclical is devoted to spelling out various aspects of the active side of this spirituality – how it is to be lived out in the economic, political and cultural spheres. I shall limit myself here to treating the contemplative dimension of the spirituality which he invites us to adopt.

Francis is calling us to quite a radical alternative to the activism which is so characteristic of Western Christian spirituality. He invites us to be fully present to nature, to the scenery and the seasons, to the lilies of the field and the birds of the air (226). The spirituality he calls for is one which enables us to 'be serenely present to each reality' (222) – and this includes each person whom we meet. As he says, 'We are speaking of an attitude of the heart, one which approaches life with serene attentiveness, which is capable of being fully present to someone without thinking of what comes next' (226). He makes a very explicit link between our relationship with people and with other creatures: 'A sense of deep communion with the rest of nature cannot be real if our hearts lack tenderness, compassion and concern for our fellow human beings' (91).

In Francis' view, the attitude that many people have today is one in which they approach other creatures in a confrontational way, trying to squeeze them dry (106). But Francis, taking St Francis as his 'guide and inspiration' (10), invites us instead to see everything in creation 'as a gift from the outstretched hand of the Father of all' (76). He takes up this notion of gift in several places in the encyclical (cf. 5, 71, 146, 155, 159, 220, 226, 227). He even suggests that we should have the kind of relationship that St Francis had with nature – like the life-changing experience one has when one falls in love with somebody (cf. 11).

It is important to note that the contemplative attitude which Francis is calling for is not simply a matter of looking on in admiration at the world around us. It also includes engaging in manual work as the monks have done for the past fifteen hundred years. Recalling St Benedict's proposal that his monks combine prayer and spiritual reading with manual work, Francis says:

> Seeing manual labour as spiritually meaningful proved revolutionary. Personal growth and sanctification came to be sought in the interplay of recollection and work. This way of experiencing work makes us more protective and respectful of the environment; it imbues our relationship to the world with a healthy sobriety. (126)

Franciscan Mysticism

As I have already noted, the encyclical puts great emphasis on the importance of experiencing the creatures of the world around us as gifts from God. He spells this out in a beautiful passage:

> This conversion calls for a number of attitudes which together foster a spirit of generous care, full of tenderness. First, it entails gratitude and gratuitousness, a recognition that the world is God's loving gift, and that we are called quietly to imitate his generosity in self-sacrifice and good works ... As believers, we do not look at the world from without but from within, conscious of the bonds with which the Father has linked us to all beings. (220)

The effect is that we experience 'a serene harmony with creation', where we are no longer clogged up by 'frenetic activity' (225). This brings about a liberation from worries and calculations about the future or the past. We are able to avoid the busyness and the 'constant flood of new consumer goods [which] can baffle the heart and prevent us from cherishing each thing and each moment' (222; cf. 113). We can really hear the words of Jesus: 'do not worry, saying, "What shall we eat?" or "What shall we drink?" or "What shall we wear?"' (Mt 6:31).

The mystical attitude which Francis advocates makes us more keenly aware that non-human creatures also praise God, each in its own way. As the encyclical points out, 'The Psalms ... also invite other creatures to join us in this praise: "Praise him, sun and moon, praise him, all you shining stars! Praise him, you highest heavens, and you waters above the heavens! Let them praise the name of the Lord"' (72).

God in the Gifts

In his adoption of this kind of Franciscan mysticism, Pope Francis goes further: he invites us not merely to see the creatures around us as gifts from God, but also to actually *experience God in the gifts.* This means that our contact with each of the people and the non-human creatures around us can be a key way of coming into touch with God. Francis says:

> The universe unfolds in God, who fills it completely. Hence, there is a mystical meaning to be found in a leaf, in a mountain trail, in a dewdrop, in a poor person's face. The ideal is not only to pass from the exterior to the interior to discover the action of God in the soul, but also to *discover God in all things.* (233, emphasis added)

This statement of Francis reminds us of the words of Mechtild of Magdeburg: 'The day of my spiritual awakening was the day I saw – and knew that I saw – God in all things and all things in God.'

The ideal to which we are called is one where we lift up our voices, in the words of St Francis of Assisi, in praise not only of the gifts with which we are surrounded but also of God, the one whom we experience, in a greater or lesser degree, *with* these gifts of nature and also *through* them:

> 'Praised be you, my Lord, *with* all your creatures … *through* Sister Moon and the stars, and *through* the air, cloudy and serene, and every kind of weather.' (87, emphasis added)

Theological Basis for an Ecological Conversion

Francis maintains that 'living our vocation to be protectors of God's handiwork is essential to a life of virtue; it is not an optional or a secondary aspect of our Christian experience'. This comes immediately after he points out that 'some committed and prayerful Christians, with the excuse of realism and pragmatism, tend to ridicule expressions of concern for the environment. Others are passive; they choose not to change their habits and thus become inconsistent' (217). Francis is quite insistent that such attitudes are simply incompatible with being a genuine Christian. Referring to those who hold these mistaken views he says, 'what they all need is an "ecological conversion", whereby the effects of their encounter with Jesus Christ become evident in their relationship with the world around them' (217).

Francis says that it would be a mistake 'to view other living beings as mere objects subjected to arbitrary human domination' (82). He speaks out against what is called 'anthropocentrism'; that is, an attitude that puts humans so much at the centre of creation that we are believed to be the only creatures who have value in their own right, and all other creatures are valued only to the extent to which they are useful to us. Francis says, 'Modernity has been marked by an excessive anthropocentrism'. He acknowledges that 'an inadequate presentation of Christian anthropology gave rise to a wrong understanding of the relationship between human beings and the world' (116).

Rejecting this human-centred approach, Francis insists that 'we are called to recognise that other living beings have a value of their own in God's eyes' (69); and he says that in slightly different ways in several other passages of the encyclical (33, 115, 118, 140, 190). Lest anybody suggest that in saying this he is not in accord with previous Catholic teaching, he goes on to quote the *Catechism of the Catholic Church* in support of what he is saying (cf. 69).

Biblical Basis

Francis puts forward the biblical foundation for an ecological conversion in theology by looking at key texts in the Book of Genesis and other parts of the Bible. He says, 'Although it is true that we Christians have at times incorrectly interpreted the Scriptures, nowadays we must forcefully reject the notion that our being created in God's image and given dominion over the earth justifies absolute domination over other creatures' (67). So he holds that a true understanding of the biblical text gives no grounds for us to engage in an 'unbridled exploitation of nature'.

In the Book of Genesis, Francis finds the basis for a correct relationship between humans and the rest of nature:

> **[The biblical texts] tell us to 'till and keep' the garden of the world (cf. Gen 2:15). 'Tilling' refers to cultivating, ploughing or working, while 'keeping' means caring, protecting, overseeing and preserving. This implies a relationship of mutual responsibility between human beings and nature. Each community can take from the bounty of the earth whatever it needs for subsistence, but it also has the duty to protect the earth and to ensure its fruitfulness for coming generations. (67)**

In the encyclical Francis notes that the biblical account of the Sabbath throws an important light on how we humans should relate to other creatures. The words of Exodus 23:12 make it clear that 'rest on the seventh day is meant not only for human beings, but also so "that your ox and your donkey may have rest"' (68). Francis also quotes a particularly moving passage from Deuteronomy (22:4–6): 'If you chance to come upon a bird's nest in any tree or on the ground, with young ones or eggs and the mother sitting upon the young or upon the eggs; you shall not take the mother with the young' (68).

Pope Francis also turns to the New Testament to find a basis for his ecological theology. He rejects the 'unhealthy dualisms which left a mark on certain Christian thinkers in the course of history and disfigured the Gospel'. He points out that Jesus lived in harmony with creation and 'was far removed from philosophies which despised the body, matter and the things of the world ... Jesus worked with his hands, in daily contact with the matter created by God, to which he gave form by his craftsmanship'. (98)

Francis points out that 'the destiny of all creation is bound up with the mystery of Christ, present from the beginning: "All things have been created through him and for him" (Col 1:16)' (99). We can say that the Word of God is already present in every aspect of creation from the beginning and that this presence comes to consciousness in some limited degree when, after billions of years, humans appear on the stage of creation. But this consciousness is mostly implicit and inadequately articulated until the coming of Jesus who is the definitive presence of God in our world and the fulfilment of all that had gone before. As Pope Francis, quoting St Paul, says: in Jesus 'the fullness of God was pleased to dwell' (Col 1:19).

In that same sentence of the letter to the Colossians, the writer says that God has brought peace and reconciliation to all of creation by the death of Jesus on the Cross. Francis maintains that this directs our gaze to the end of time when the risen Jesus has brought his work of salvation to completion and 'the Son will deliver all things to the Father'. The point Francis is making is that what is reconciled and handed over to God is not just humanity but all of creation. And so he can say that *already* the risen Jesus is mysteriously holding all creatures to himself 'and directing them towards fullness as their end' (100). So, the hope of Christians is directed not just to personal resurrection or to the resurrection of the human community but also to a 'new earth' which will be the redemption and fulfilment of this present creation of which we are an integral part.

Sacramental Theology

There is an important ecological aspect to Catholic sacramental theology. This, too, can be taken in under the term 'integral ecology'. Francis says:

> **The Sacraments are a privileged way in which nature is taken up by God to become a means of mediating supernatural life. ... Water, oil, fire and colours are taken up in all their symbolic power and incorporated in our act of praise. (235)**

He goes on to spell this out in some detail in his account of the Eucharist, in which 'all that has been created finds its greatest exaltation'. He points out that Jesus comes to us 'not from above, but from within, he comes that we might find him in this world of ours' (235). The point that Francis is making is that the presence of Jesus in the Eucharist is, so to speak, an extension of the Incarnation of Jesus. Jesus took on our flesh, being born of a human mother and having a body composed of the same material as ours – the star stuff that emerged from the Big Bang billions of years ago. So the material of the Eucharist is all the food of our everyday world. As editor Sean Mc Donagh says, the bread and wine 'represent crops and vineyards, sunshine and rain, the God given bounty of the earth'. And they combine 'the fertility of the earth ... with human creativity, in farming, baking, cultivation of vines and wine-making ... "work of human hands."'[4] So Francis says that 'Eucharist is itself an act of cosmic love ... a source of light and motivation for our concerns for the environment, directing us to be stewards of all creation' (236).

Francis goes on to lay particular emphasis on the celebration of Eucharist on a Sunday, because every Sunday 'is meant to be a day which heals our relationships with God, with ourselves, with others and with the world'. The Sabbath as a day of rest 'incorporates the value of relaxation and festivity' as well as 'receptivity and gratuity' into Christian spirituality. In this way it 'protects human action from becoming empty activism ... and motivates us to greater concern for nature and the poor' (237).

I hope that this account of some elements in the encyclical will encourage people to read the document for themselves and to appreciate the richness and complexity of the 'ecological conversion' which Pope Francis is calling for. Even more importantly, I hope that it will encourage them to respond positively to the invitation of Francis, and to take on the challenge of allowing themselves to be ecologically converted.

Endnotes

1. Address of Pope Francis to the Participants in the World Meeting of Popular Movements, 28 October 2014, w2.vatican.va/content/francesco/en/speeches/2014/october/documents/papa-francesco_20141028_incontro-mondiale-movimenti-popolari.html; Address of Pope Francis to the Participants at the Second World Meeting of Popular Movements, 9 July 2015, w2.vatican.va/content/francesco/en/speeches/2015/july/documents/papa-francesco_20150709_bolivia-movimenti-popolari.html.

2. I have written an extended account of all of these different aspects of the encyclical in the new edition of my book *Option for the Poor and for the Earth*, New York: Orbis Books, 2016.

3. See, for instance, Thomas Berry, *The Dream of the Earth*, San Francisco: Sierra Club Books, 1988, pp. 124–36.

4. Sean McDonagh, *On Care for Our Common Home*, New York: Orbis Books, 2016, pp. 118–20.

Demography, Poverty and Planetary Boundaries in *Laudato Si'*

CATHRIONA RUSSELL

The weeks after the release of *Laudato Si'* were marked, it is said, by predictable reactions: approval from the environmental movement; rejection from parts of the conservative mainstream media; and a deafening silence from the so-called climate skeptics.[1] It is unprecedented in the history of Catholic social teaching for renowned scientific journals *Nature* and *Science* to publish favourable editorials before and after the publication of an encyclical.[2] But the problems too are unprecedented, and the encyclical both mirrors and endorses calls that we become 'active stewards of our own life supports system' exactly because we 'are the first generation with the knowledge of how our activities influence the Earth System, and thus the first generation with the power and the responsibility to change our relationship with the planet'.[3]

This chapter begins with a brief presentation of the encyclical from the perspective of ethics and environmental theology, before turning its approach to demography, which is the central theme.

The reception of paragraph fifty in particular, which focusses on demographic growth, has been remarkable in its breadth. Yet, when we examine some of the commonly held assumptions about the relationship between demographics and planetary boundaries – specifically climate change and the loss of biodiversity – it seems safe to conclude that paragraph fifty is measured and prudent.

Ethics and Environmental Theology in *Laudato Si'*

Laudato Si' embodies an example of the learning Church at its best; in relation to our common home, it says, we need dialogue between men and women, Christian churches, all faiths, and all people of good will. It has been noted for its demonstration of collegiality within the Church, quoting bishops' conferences from Latin America and Asia, the Caribbean, Germany, Japan, Brazil, Paraguay, New Zealand, Argentina, Portugal and Australia. It champions a model of dialogue, defending the cultural riches of different peoples, their art and poetry, their interior life and spirituality. And it is inviting in relation to all disciplines when it acknowledges that no branch of the sciences and no form of wisdom can be left out in caring for our common home.

The encyclical also expresses an appreciation of creation that is far from formulaic, referring, as St Francis of Assisi did, to that other book of revelation, the Book of Nature (cf. 12), to creation as God's art (cf. 81), to a sublime fraternity in creation (cf. 22) and creation as a caress of God (cf. 84). The earth is the creation that was here before us (cf. 66), our homeland (cf. 164). There is sacramentality in a leaf (cf. 223) and every sparrow counts (cf. 96). The creator never forsakes his plan or repents of having created (cf. 13), each of us is loved, each of us is necessary (cf. 65), all creatures are moving forward with us and through us (cf. 83), and God is intimately present (cf. 80).

For many scientists and economists, the encyclical also exhibits a well-informed expertise in relation to the concrete issues. It coins a new word, 'rapidification', as shorthand for the underlying symptom, something that is contrasted with the pace of evolutionary biology (cf. 18). It is also very specific in defining the problems (cf. 57): flooding; water privatisation; the loss of biodiversity; the excluded millions; the minority that currently consume in a way that can never be universalised; the irrational application of inappropriate technology; the ravages of war; and the impact all of these have not only on the environment but also on the cultural riches of peoples.[4]

In terms of how we should act, the encyclical has set some interesting ground rules, most significantly that we all have common, but also differentiated, responsibilities (cf. 169).[5] This is accompanied by many models drawn from the Christian tradition and beyond: the ascetic idea of learning to give, not simply giving up (cf. 9); that each of us does this creatively according to his or her own culture, experience, involvements and talents (cf. 14); that our traditions can render our commitment to the environment more coherent (cf. 15) and not tiresome and abstract (cf. 17); that there are ecological virtues (cf. 88) but that we also have duties to each other as people and all creatures (cf. 92); and that it is life, recreation and community and not consumerism that are liberating (cf. 112).

There is a stress too on the value of work (cf. 124), as distinct from paid employment (cf. 180); indeed for some this is the message at the heart of the letter as a social encyclical.[6] And it is encouraging that it describes the 1992 UN Earth Summit in Rio de Janeiro as 'prophetic for its time' and for several well-thought-out reasons. Rio acknowledged that the human person should be at the centre of the concern for sustainable development; that there was a need to reverse the trend in global warming. It also drew up a convention on biodiversity and principles regarding forests – even if those 'principles that it proclaimed still await an efficient and flexible means of practical implementation' (166).

Demography in *Laudato Si'*

The encyclical endorses approaches that keep the human person at the centre of concerns for the planet. It does not begin, therefore, as some might have preferred, with an analysis from the point of view of population growth or with controversies and conflicts within the religions about contraception and family. Its primary references to humanity are much more apt: care for the human family in relation to environmental risks and hazards; concern for the cultural impact of pollution and flooding; for access to clean water; for the related health of animal populations; for food security from the sea; and for the millions excluded from enjoying a good quality of life. It takes issue with the reduction of workers to productive units or collateral damage in the global economy, and the lack of social contact that can be driven by the disintegration of our cities. It is not controversial, merely descriptive, when it concludes as follows: it 'needs to be said that, generally speaking, there is little in the way of clear awareness of problems which especially affect the excluded. Yet they are the majority of the planet's population, billions of people.' (49)

The extent and causes of global poverty are well documented and complex. I would recommend the work of the health statistician Hans Rosling and his *Gapminder* resource for an analysis of population growth and poverty alleviation in the last two hundred years. Rosling's work 'minds the gap' between popular perception and the reality of human demographics, and his presentation of the data is a resource for planners and policy makers alike.[7] Poverty, too, however it is measured, cannot simply be characterised as a problem of lack of resources but is a lack of entitlement, something likewise well documented and explored by the development economist and moral philosopher Amartya Sen. Sen's series of lectures at the World Bank in 1996, later published under the title of *Development as Freedom* in 1999, have radically reshaped the debate and policy on the relationship between sustainable growth and human development.[8] His analysis of the Irish Famine in the nineteenth century and his personal experience of famine in India in his boyhood, the Bengal Famine in 1943, provide part of the evidence base for his economic approach. Prosperity in Sen's model is rooted in the capability for people to 'live lives they have reason to value' and is not simply measured in terms of rising GDP. The encyclical champions a model of development rooted in the Church's 'preferential option for the poor' in the first instance and the international consensus that there are links between a stable planet and human welfare that cannot be ignored.

Demography: Population Growth and Consumerism

Despite this overarching concern for humanity and the planet, the very few and carefully worded paragraphs on population growth have engendered some heated political and theological debate from very diverse groups. The significant paragraph, paragraph fifty, says:

> Instead of resolving the problems of the poor and thinking of how the world can be different, some can only propose a reduction in the birth rate. At times, developing countries face forms of international pressure, which make economic assistance contingent on certain policies of 'reproductive health'. Yet 'while it is true that an unequal distribution of

the population and of available resources creates obstacles to development and a sustainable use of the environment, it must nonetheless be recognised that demographic growth is fully compatible with an integral and shared development'.[9] To blame population growth instead of extreme and selective consumerism on the part of some is one way of refusing to face the issues. It is an attempt to legitimise the present model of distribution, where a minority believes that it has the right to consume in a way which can never be universalised, since the planet could not even contain the waste products of such consumption. Besides, we know that approximately a third of all food produce is discarded ... Still, attention needs to be paid to imbalances in population density, on both national and global levels, since a rise in consumption would lead to complex regional situations, as a result of the interplay between problems linked to environmental pollution, transport, waste treatment, loss of resources and quality of life.

The use of 'demography' in referring to human societies is a welcome move away from an exclusive use of 'population', a term that belongs well enough in ecology but is not apt in politics and social policy, carrying as it does the baggage of past failed and undemocratic social engineering projects (projects that have been referred to as versions of 'social Darwinism'). This welcome shift in the discourse is also quietly reflected in the framing of international assessments on development. In the UN's recent report *Population and Sustainable Development in the Post-2015 Agenda* (2014) the two overarching messages are listed as: 'demography matters for sustainable development' and 'demography is not destiny'.[10] In contrast, the earlier report in 2012 uses 'population matters' and 'population is not destiny'.[11]

Responses to Paragraph Fifty: Too Much, Too Little, or Just Right?

Paragraph fifty has prompted some rather surprising and diverging reactions in theological circles and beyond. The most counter-rational, monster of a response was from Steve Jalsevac of the Canadian news site, *Lifesite*. This describes itself as a non-profit internet service dedicated to issues of culture, life, and family.[12] Jalsevac, the co-founder and managing director of that site, states that:

> [The] extent of the laudatory comments from President Obama, UN leaders, all the liberal mainstream media, almost all leading Catholic dissidents and other of the most prominent world de-population, anti-Christian, socialist and even Marxist leaders, is chilling for those who understand the implications of this extraordinary support for the encyclical.[13]

This alarm, he argues, is especially felt among 'pro-life, pro-family leaders who have been working since 1994 at the UN in response to a special appeal from Pope John Paul II'.[14] For Jalsevac, this rather short and circumspect paragraph, rather than being a clear restatement of Catholic social teaching on the dignity of the person and the family, is just grist for the neo-Malthusian mill.

Admittedly, the spectre of social Darwinism has not entirely departed, even if the discourse has softened. The NGO Population Matters, formerly the Optimum Population Trust, recently argued for cutting child supports for 'third and subsequent children' and for 'zero-net-migration' of refugees to the UK (one in, one out).[15] This NGO has some high profile patrons, the broadcaster and naturalist David Attenborough, the primatologist Jane Goodall and most recently the actor Joanna Lumley. Nevertheless, it too has its critics and these are not only from theological circles. Open Democracy, a very different global media platform, based on the other side of the Atlantic, in Britain this time, raises similar questions about popular assumptions in relation to population growth, but from a very different starting point. It claims not moral theology but human rights as its guiding focus and takes issue with NGOs that promote a 'neo-Malthusian' agenda. The concern for human dignity and freedom in the context of neo-colonial development agendas cuts across the so-called Church–secular divide and *Laudato Si'* could never be interpreted as suggesting that humanity is a plague, as Attenborough has recently done.[16]

There is more than one way to evaluate the data on demographics, but the narrative that poor countries, where population growth is most rapid, are the immediate problem, does not stand up. Currently about 7 per cent of the world's population is responsible for 50 per cent of greenhouse gas emissions. This can look even more damning if you count from the beginning of the Great Acceleration, dated by Steffen et al. to the beginning of the industrial revolution, 1751. From that perspective, it is the wealthiest countries that account then for 80 per cent of the total emissions and the 'world's poorest countries … have contributed less than 1 per cent'.[17]

There were certainly those who reacted negatively to the encyclical's 'silence on population growth', seeing it as a lost opportunity to lift the ban on artificial contraception, much debated since *Humanae Vitae* (1968). Graham Brown, professor in international development in the University of Western Australia, says that the 'gaping hole' in *Laudato Si'* is 'the issue of population and population growth' and the silence on this is 'damaging and dangerous'.[18] In his analysis of what he calls the false dichotomy between consumerism and population he laments what he sees as the letter's position that 'unchecked population growth is commensurate with equitable and sustainable development'. Paragraph fifty, however, does not refer to 'unchecked' population growth. Instead, it insists on a better basis for talking about people and their societies, and points to the chief driver of environmental damage: consumerism.

It is undoubtedly necessary to examine under what conditions it is possible to talk of growth and shared development, but much depends on what kind of growth is envisaged: is it the model of material opulence that we currently tolerate, or resilience, flexibility and creativity, uncoupled from greenhouse gas emissions and consumerism? Brown, however, is correct – contra *Lifesite* – that this encyclical is not arguing for a shift from a traditional defense of the family, in particular in relation to the freedom to negotiate the question of family size. Under the principle of subsidiarity, it is the family and not the state or even the 'greater common good' that is the competent locus in this regard.

It is also the case that the internal Church debates about demography and the moral teaching on birth control are by no means without subtleties or are simply settled in one direction. As Sean McDonagh, Columban priest and eco-theologian, observes in his book on *Laudato Si'*, previous encyclicals clearly recognised that accelerated population growth can pose problems for development.[19] McDonagh does argue that in the light of a 'demographic crisis' the Church should 'revisit its teaching on birth control'.[20] He is not alone in that, and not only because of environmental questions but also for the sake of families. And the Catholic world and communities have already developed a nuanced *sensus fidelium* on this question that cannot fail to be instructive. The current pope's recent comments, although a little too rustic for the sensibilities of some, reflect an awareness of just that.[21]

There is no doubt that social pressure to contain family size to 'replacement' levels can be coercive and that large families can be wonderful. On the other hand it would be wayward and likewise coercive to make large families a Catholic status symbol or a mark of superior piety.[22] Hans Rosling's work is instructive here, it shows that 'responsible parenting' across religions and cultures is already visible in the statistics. In his *Religion and Babies* TED Talk, he says 'all the religions in the world are fully capable of maintaining their values and adopt to this new world': we have reached 'peak child', he argues, and the world population will stabilise at around ten billion people.[23] And even if the world's population was to stop growing this year, the problems of current unsustainable consumption by the wealthiest 7 per cent should be vastly more emphasised than population numbers.

There are also other relevant trends in relation to demographics, particularly if we look at the disaggregated data. In some countries the population is falling, or the growth rate is at or below replacement level and it is inward migration that supports these economies.[24] In addition, the 'democratic dividend' (the economic benefits that come with a shift in age structures) that could still accrue to developing countries if wisely managed, cannot be discounted, especially if those countries leapfrog to more sustainable resource use.

The onus is on those who claim to be concerned about population growth to show how they promote – and indeed seek public funding for – policies that increase and do not diminish the freedoms and capabilities of all humanity to 'live lives we have reason to value'. Otherwise their policies remain unconvincing, and self-serving at best.

There are gaps in the data, and a need for new networks of knowledge to show how demographics, poverty and planetary boundaries are related beyond the masking assumptions about sheer numbers alone. We cannot simply assume a correlation between demography and poverty, nor between population and other planetary boundaries.[25] In the next section I will explore some of the relationships that have been traced between these.

Demography and Poverty Alleviation

Amartya Sen wrote in the 1990s that in recent decades the population problem has been increasingly presented as a bomb, already planted and about to go off. These 'catastrophic images', he says, 'have encouraged a tendency to search for emergency solutions which treat the people involved not as reasonable beings, allies facing a common problem, but as impulsive and uncontrolled sources of great social harm, in need of strong discipline.'[26]

Yet he demonstrates that in country after country, with development, the birth rate has steadied and this stabilisation in demographics has clear drivers directly related to poverty alleviation strategies. These are now well recognised: education for girls and women; the reduction in child mortality rates; the expansion of economic means and security; and greater public discussion of ways of living. He has also demonstrated that coercive methods, whether direct (one child policy) or indirect (through taxation and withholding of essential services) have not been more successful than the four factors above in comparable time frames. Indeed there is evidence to suggest that coercive methods, even apart from their negative impact on gender balance and the care of infant girls, which is already a great loss of freedom, may well be counterproductive in maintaining that steadied growth, now at 'replacement' across much of the globe.[27] The Malthusian prediction that fertility rates would increase exponentially the more prosperous societies became has been discredited.[28]

The global human population is no longer growing exponentially. The most recent UN report sets the global population peak at just over eleven billion, based on revised predictions.[29] There are uncertainties about when we will reach certain demographic milestones, partly because of unreliable statistics but also because of 'inherent uncertainty about future rates of fertility, mortality, and migration'.[30] Scherbov et al. argue that population forecasts should, but do not always, adequately reflect these uncertainties and there needs to be more transparency about presuppositions. Nevertheless, they calculate that there is a high chance that the eight billion milestone will be reached between 2022 and 2035. There is also little uncertainty that the world's population will peak, and start to decline before the end of the century.[31]

Other important factors, apart from population size, are at work in relation to poverty. A useful analysis of the correlation between development and population growth is by no means straightforward and the global trend is uneven, as *Laudato Si'* recognises. Indeed, Sen argues that to see all the causal factors of deprivation, rural or urban, as a result of overpopulation is the negation of social analysis and is not empirically convincing.[32] There are many causal factors, and population growth itself, for example, does not help to:

> explain why the slums of Calcutta and Bombay have grown worse at a faster rate than those of Karachi and Islamabad (India's population growth rate is 2.1 percent per year, Pakistan's 3.1), or why Jakarta has deteriorated faster than Ankara or Istanbul (Indonesian population growth is 1.8 percent, Turkey's 2.3), or why the slums of Mexico City have become worse more rapidly than those of San José (Mexico's population growth rate is 2.0, Costa Rica's 2.8), or why Harlem can seem more deprived when compared with the poorer districts of Singapore (US population growth rate is 1.0, Singapore's is 1.8).[33]

There is no simple relationship between poverty and demographics, although poverty alleviation 'derapidifies' population growth. Coercive policies, direct or indirect, under the banner of 'reproductive responsibility' are not a route to population stabilisation, and population stabilisation, without capability building, is not a direct route to poverty alleviation. Neither will population stabilisation decouple growth from carbon emissions. Other factors play a greater role in our living within the boundaries of the planet.

If we assume that the planetary boundaries concept is a useful way to express environmental problems we can argue that the earth's carrying capacity is being exceeded in relation to at least three boundaries: climate change, the nitrogen cycle and biodiversity loss.[34] I will now examine the links between population and climate change in the first instance and poverty and biodiversity conservation in the second.

Demography and Climate Change

Despite the advances in combating hunger and the establishment and arguably even the attainment of some of the millennium development goals, 'there is growing evidence that Western production and consumption patterns are not generalisable to the rest of the planet if environmental concerns are considered'.[35] Living off the earth's natural capital can and has lead to improvements in human welfare but this cannot be sustained indefinitely.[36] The provisioning goods, supporting and regulating services, or Earth System Services (ESS) are in decline, even as the Human Development Index (HDI) continues to increase.

How is this related to demographics? The first thing to acknowledge is that the main cause of climate change is overwhelmingly consumption in developed countries, the countries where, ironically, 'population growth has been low or negative'.[37] Climate change is not a function of population size and it is more accurate to say, as *Laudato Si'* states, that 'climate change is driven more by consumer behaviour than simply by population number'.[38] Therefore, under present conditions, in which the developed and overdeveloped economies 'do not radically reduce their carbon emissions', advocating reduced population growth in developing countries, especially as a condition for development, risks victimising the victims.[39]

However, humanity does face enormous challenges in achieving climate-sustainable emissions. And developing countries are faced with even greater challenges because the:

> pathways of development followed by today's wealthy countries after the Second World War – built on plentiful, cheap fossil fuel energy resources, an abundance of other material resources, and large expanses of productive land being developed – cannot be followed by the 75–80 per cent of the human population who are at various stages on their trajectories out of poverty, and are beginning to compete with today's wealthy countries for increasingly scarce natural resources.[40]

It is too easily taken as a given that population growth drives increasing emissions. Again, the picture is complex. Since the beginning of the industrial revolution, human population has tripled, but also in that same time 'the global economy and material consumption has grown many times faster'.[41] Consumption outstrips population growth by several factors. In addition, if you separate out the aggregated data for population it reveals that 'consumption in the OECD countries, rather than population growth in the rest of the world, has been the more important driver of change during the Great Acceleration, including the most recent decade'.[42]

There is evidence too that development can follow alternative patterns; some non-OECD countries have managed to leapfrog rich countries in their use of key technologies for development; for example, mobile phone networks in Africa and Asia have now bypassed the need to install landline infrastructure. Development can be decoupled from high-emissions infrastructure.

It is, of course, another matter altogether to leapfrog energy intensive pathways that are dependent on fossil fuel in order to decouple greenhouse gas emissions from economic growth.[43] Nevertheless, it is possible to imagine other models, because other models of development already exist. We can conclude both that the contribution to carbon emissions that low-income, high-fertility countries have made to date is negligible, and that poor and developing countries need not follow the same trajectories as the industrialised world as they develop their economies in order to reduce poverty and increase human well-being.[44]

If we do plan to keep the earth in a state conducive to further human development[45] and make the transition to a global economy that respects earth boundaries, one of the challenges is to establish new measures of prosperity that include ecological sustainability, social inclusion, human well-being and quality of life.[46] New economic policies have been developed for poverty alleviation for only a handful of decades but with some considerable success. There are models to draw on. Amartya Sen's capability approach has generated practical and effective alternative ways to measure prosperity that improve poverty alleviation strategies. These are being applied in ways that point to mechanisms that can decouple carbon emissions from prosperity. Sen's work has produced new perspectives on social choice theory in relation to poverty alleviation that moves us away from the 'satisfaction of needs' approach to 'freedoms to act', which can include acting for the sake of healthy environments. We also need new models of human flourishing and prosperity that can conceive in terms not just of underdevelopment and development but also of overdevelopment.

Underdevelopment, Development and Overdevelopment

The social scientists Martin Fritz and Max Koch identify prosperity patterns in groups of counties currently at different states of development; the first group of thirty-two is made up of poor countries with what they refer to as 'factor-driven' economies. These countries have little choice but to try to establish the basic requirements of socio-economic development. This list includes Uganda, Chad, Afghanistan, Bangladesh and Myanmar. Here, ecological sustainability can deteriorate with the building of infrastructure and sale of natural resources.[47] The thirty-three developing countries they classify as having 'efficiency-driven' economies include Angola, Ghana, Nigeria, Bolivia, Ecuador, Jamaica, Nicaragua, Bosnia and Ukraine. Their increasing expansion of consumption will have a negative impact on their ecological performance under current conditions. The third group contains thirty-three countries with emerging economies that exceed subsistence levels but are not always growing in terms of GDP. The fourth group – the rich economies – is 'innovation-driven'. Through improvements in efficiency (not effectiveness) they have experienced, but are not now accompanied by, further environmental degradation.[48] This group includes many of the advanced OECD countries of Europe. Lastly, there are eight countries that are classified as 'overdeveloped', who have extraordinarily high material standards of living. These are an elite set of oil-exporting states (e.g. Kuwait and Norway), financial hubs (e.g. Singapore and Switzerland) and include the world's largest economy (USA).[49]

How does each fare in terms of emissions and prosperity indicators? Ecological impact rises from one level of development to the next and only the poorest (and most populous) are close to environmentally 'sustainable'.[50] There is, similarly, an increase in political freedoms and democratic structures from the least developed to the rich countries, but this is uneven and does not always follow for the overdeveloped countries.[51] Overall, current models of economic development enhance social inclusion and quality of life but at the expense of the environment. Not a promising picture for protecting planetary boundaries.

However, Fritz and Koch also show that other patterns are possible, and that some countries exhibit prosperity beyond growth (or perhaps before) growth.[52] Some emerging economies, for example, Costa Rica and Panama, exhibit a relative decoupling of emissions from prosperity.[53] Even where developing economies are counted as being high emitters, the metrics can leave out connections between countries in terms of global trading patterns. The stabilising of emissions claimed for developed countries, like Ireland and many countries of the EU, is made possible through imports from the manufacturing developing countries.[54]

This analysis throws up some other relevant patterns in the emissions narrative. Territorial-based emissions metrics show China as the largest global emitter with the US in second place. Much is made of this in the popular media. However, consumption-based inventory reverses this order, and it is the US that is counted as the largest emitter. Peters et al. also show that most developed countries, including EU countries, move up the emissions ranking with consumption-based metrics.[55] The larger macroeconomic imbalances in the world economy – imbalances that are unrelated to climate policy – already frame and constrain that policy. Clearly, additional modelling for policy formation is required.[56]

If we argue for contraction and convergence to reduce carbon emissions to a sustainable or equitable level,[57] and political global agreement on emissions is taken seriously, the policy challenges would be different for each of these groups of countries. This echoes the *UN Framework Convention on Climate Change* and *Laudato Si'*: we have common but differentiated responsibilities and it is consumer patterns that are critical (and not population).

Demography and Biodiversity Conservation

The second planetary boundary that has been exceeded is biodiversity, which refers not to availability, abundance or biomass, but to variability.[58] Although notoriously difficult to evaluate, there is a general consensus that this variability contributes to ecosystem provisioning services and to well-being. It is also an important indicator of the integrity of the global environment, and is said to secure ecosystem resilience.[59] There is no dispute that we are currently experiencing a mass extinction of life that is anthropogenic and that the earth's biodiversity is immediately endangered by human activity.[60]

Practitioners link biodiversity loss with poverty, and, as we have seen already, poverty is linked to population growth.[61] Development brings population stabilisation but the impact on biodiversity conservation is uneven and not clearly related to either alleviation or population size. The poor countries contribute to biodiversity loss, but so do all economies (overdeveloped, rich, emerging, developing). However, it seems the poor are also burdened with the perception that they are 'undermining conservation' and that the bigger the population, the greater the problem.[62] There are plenty of examples of this correlation; McDonagh cites the case of the Philippines where he worked for many decades. Its population has grown to one hundred million in the last century and in that time almost all of its primary forest cover has been logged.[63] This is a tragic loss but then deforestation is not new. Europe and the Middle East were converted in past centuries from their original cover and almost all the old growth forests in the US were already cut by the

1920s. If we are to conserve biodiversity reserves and hotspots, we need to learn from past mistakes by first acknowledging them.

In addition, if we look more closely, and disaggregate the data, governance factors are more significant predictors of loss than the constraints of geography and population. The marginalisation of poor people is not new, nor is it specific to conservation.[64] It is, nonetheless, depressing to find Billé et al. conclude as follows in their otherwise nuanced presentation: 'While fighting poverty is undoubtedly a noble cause, setting it as a global sustainability priority is a choice that may need to be debated, at least when it comes to biodiversity conservation.'[65] The question immediately arises as to who gets to participate in the decision-making on these vital questions.

We do need a 'clearer articulation of the links between biodiversity and agriculture and between biodiversity and ecosystem services'.[66] There are existing models of conservation and examples of reconstruction of habitats that are consistent with prosperity but they are as yet fragmented. These include, but are not confined to, nature-based tourism, agroforestry and agro-biodiversity conservation.[67] The European Commission's adoption of the concept of a 'circular economy' may also prove to be a more consistent policy for conservation.[68] *Laudato Si'* refers to the good practices but acknowledges that they are far from widespread (57).

There is one other vital ingredient emerging in the evidence base, where researchers have cared to look for it. According to Billé et al., biodiversity loss in all economies is more directly related to inequality than it is to poverty or, by implication, population. The best predictor of a threatened species includes not just economic footprint but also inequality (outperforming population density alone). These authors claim that inequalities 'are likely to be the fundamental missing piece of the biodiversity-poverty puzzle, finally putting coherence in fragmented observations that, for instance, poverty is a cause of biodiversity erosion while clearly wealth is an even greater one'.[69]

Poverty alleviation does 'derapidify' population growth but inequality alleviation is needed to decelerate the loss of species and consolidate biodiversity conservation. There are those who would argue that reducing inequalities is not a legitimate economic or social objective,[70] and others that would argue that increasing GDP is the best mechanism to achieving it. The evidence suggests, however, that we cannot ignore the impact of socioeconomic inequality as 'an important factor to consider when predicting rates of anthropogenic biodiversity loss'.[71]

Demography is Not Destiny

Demography matters but is not destiny. Linking population growth with climate change and biodiversity loss is not a simple matter. Population dynamics do need to be integrated into climate science but in a way that takes account of not only growth but also migration, urbanisation, ageing and household composition.[72] The 'synergies and positive externalities' in the relationships between population, poverty and biodiversity need to be further uncovered.[73] The picture that is emerging from the evidence base is that inequalities within and between countries present one of the greatest challenges to ensuring a 'safe operating space' for humanity. Amartya Sen's capability approach, which measures prosperity and poverty in more that the metrics of GDP, shows even more promise when it comes to biodiversity conservation. In this light, the emphasis *Laudato Si'* places on consumerism and not population is not misdirection or a false dichotomy but measured and prudent.

Elinor Ostrom, the American political economist, argued that global governance can be built on a multilevel, polycentric systems and that collective action need not wait on one international treaty.[74] *Laudato Si'* also argues for a polycentric approach, for a plurality of responses to caring for our common home; no form of wisdom can be left out including the cultural wisdom of peoples and the role of solidarity. Fritz and Koch observe that, in relation to emissions and well-being, poor and rich countries (who perform best) show similar patterns of social cohesion and governance, and these patterns are characterised by bottom-up solidarity.[75] In contrast, developing and emerging countries are characterised more by top-down conformity pressure and inequality. There are lessons here for building new networks of social cohesion for inequality alleviation as countries develop along low emissions trajectories. Not as a luxury but as that which drives the process, much like the education of women drives population stabilisation.

John Betjeman in the poem 'The Planter's Vision' parodies the hubris and homogenisation in the mechanical, single-issue vision of the future as 'worker's flats in fields of soya beans'. 'Long-sighted certainty and steerability' is important but we also need 'to focus on the short-term and inevitably messy business in which we all struggle to get more things right and fewer things wrong'.[76] We should not undermine the international commitments to justice and freedom in the name of population stability, particularly given that this will not in itself secure planetary boundaries.

Laudato Si' is not naïve about any immanent perfectibility. The encyclical talks quietly too of the 'ecology of daily life' of a 'social life that can light up a seemingly undesirable environment' (147). It provides a different vision of the future that does not leave out the possibilities and potential in a common life that can appreciate indigenous neighbourhoods where others see only slums, that applauds the irrepressible in human creativity (131) and works to create spaces, urban or otherwise, that 'connect, relate and favour the recognition of others' (152).

Endnotes

1.   Ottmar Edenhofer and Christian Flachsland, '*Laudato Si'*: 'Concern for Our Global Commons' *Thinking Faith*, 25 September 2016, p. 1.

2.   Ibid., p. 3.

3.   Will Steffen et al., 'The Anthropocene: From Global Change to Planetary Stewardship', *Ambio*, November 2011, 40:7, p. 749.

4.   It recognises the loss of biodiversity and human impacts on the integrity of earth systems (8), that climate stability is a common good (23), the earth is a shared inheritance (93), that solidarity (159), subsidiarity (196), and precaution (186) are called for. It also exhibits a competence in and awareness of the principle of ecology and examples of good practice. It comments on the difference between efficiency and effectiveness in our technological systems (22), the far-sightedness that is needed for conservation (36, 178), that some hotspots need greater protection (37), that there are no uniform remedies – that realities are greater than ideas (201), that the integrity of ecosystem and the integrity of human life are related and that the attentiveness to this universal fraternity is not something we master, nor is it contrived, but is found, uncovered (225).

5.   Cathriona Russell, 'Burden Sharing in a Changing Climate: Which Principles and Practices can Theologians Endorse?' *Studies in Christian Ethics*, 2011, 24:1, pp. 67–76.

6.   Michael Czerny, 'Neither Eco nor Green: A Social Encyclical', *Semanario Ecclesia*, 18 June 2015, laudatosi.va/content/giustiziaepace/en/speciale-laudato-si/approfondimenti/neither-_eco_-nor-green--a-social-encyclical.html

7.   Cf. gapminder.org/

8.   Sudhir Anand and Amartya Sen, 'Human Development and Economic Sustainability', *World Development* 2000, 28:12, pp. 2029–49.

9.   Quoting the *Pontifical Council for Justice and Peace, Compendium of the Social Doctrine of the Church*, 483.

10.   UNFPA, *Population and Sustainable Development in the Post-2015 Agenda*, 2014, www.unfpa.org/publications/population-and-sustainable-development-post-2015-agenda. Accessed 28 April 2016.

11.   UNFPA, *Population Matters for Sustainable Development*, 2012, www.unfpa.org/sites/default/files/pub-pdf/UNFPA%20Population%20matters%20for%20sustainable%20development_1.pdf. Accessed 28 April 2016.

12.   www.lifesitenews.com. Accessed 27 April 2016.

13.   Steve Jalsevac, 'Growing Alarm Over Francis, Encyclical *Laudato Si'*, *Lifesite*, 2 July 2015, lifesitenews.com/blogs/growing-alarm-over-dangerous-impact-of-encyclical-laudato-si. Accessed 27 April 2016.

14.   John Paul II, he writes, was then 'deeply concerned and appealed to the world's pro-life organizations to thwart efforts at the United Nations to advance a host of agendas against life and the family. Those who have heavily labored since 1994 in this international arena, constantly supported and encouraged by the Holy See delegation to the UN, are dismayed to be witnessing the Holy See now working very closely with some of the very same people they have been heroically fighting all those years. These actions are undermining the extraordinary successes of the last twenty-one years and ignoring the years of insider knowledge and experience gained about the machinations of the UN and its NGO and other allies to derail Christian civilization.'

15.   Adam Ramsey, 'The Charity which campaigned to ban Syrian Refugees from Britain', *Open Democracy UK*, opendemocracy.net/ourkingdom/adam-ramsay/charity-which-campaigned-to-ban-syrian-refugees-from-britain. Accessed 9 May 2016.

16. Louise Gray, 'David Attenborough: Humans are Plague on Earth', *The Telegraph*, 22 January 2013, telegraph.co.uk/news/earth/earthnews/9815862/Humans-are-plague-on-Earth-Attenborough.html

17. Steffen et al., 'The Antropocene', p. 746.

18. Graham Brown, 'The false dichotomy of population and consumerism in *Laudato Si'*, 20 June 2015, grahamkbrown.net/2015/06/20/the-false-dichotomy-of-population-and-consumerism-in-laudato-si/

19. Sean McDonagh, *On Care for Our Common Home: Laudato Si'*, New York: Orbis Books, 2015.

20. Sean McDonagh, *On Care for Our Common Home*, p. 66.

21. Scott Alessi, 'Pope Francis, Procreation and Rabbits', *US Catholic*, uscatholic.org/blog/201501/pope-francis-procreation-and-rabbits-29704. Accessed 9 April 2016.

22. Among rich urbanites in overdeveloped countries large families have become a status symbol, reinforcing the assumption that it is only the poor who should limit family size. Julie Zeveloff, 'The ultimate status symbol for millionaire moms on New York's Upper East Side is not what you'd expect', *Business Insider*, 25 May 2015, businessinsider.com/the-ultimate-status-symbol-is-a-big-family-2015-5?IR=T. Accessed 25 June 2016.

23. Hans Rosling, *Hans Rosling: Religion and Babies* [video] TED Talks, April 2012, ted.com/talks/hans_rosling_religions_and_babies?language=en. Accessed 14 May 2016.

24. Sean McDonagh, *On Care for Our Common Home*, p. 65.

25. Victor Galaz, 'Planetary boundaries concept is valuable', *Nature*, 2012, 486:191 doi: 10.1038/486191c. There are nine boundaries: atmospheric carbon dioxide concentration; extinction rate; nitrogen and phosphorous cycles; ocean acidification; land use; freshwater; ozone depletion; atmospheric aerosols; and chemical pollution.

26. Amartya Sen, 'Population: Delusion and Reality' in David Keller, *Environmental Ethics: The Big Questions*, Oxford: Wiley, 2010, pp. 454–468. Sen championed a new approach to development that shifted the understanding of development from economic measures of well-being alone. Development is now no longer just measured simplistically in terms of gross domestic product (GDP) but in relation to the human development index (HDI), which he helped to pioneer. This is a composite measurement, which includes life expectancy, education and income per capita as an index of development.

27. Amartya Sen, *Development as Freedom*, New York: Oxford University Press, 1999.

28. Sen, 'Population', p. 454.

29. UN Department of Economic and Social Affairs Population Division, *World Population Prospects: The 2015 Revision, Key Finding and Advanced Tables*, New York, 2015, p. 1.

30. Sergei Scherboo, Wolgang Lutz and Warren Sanderson, 'The Uncertain Timing of Reaching 8 Billion, Peak World Population, and other Demographic Milestones', *Population and Development Review*, 2011, 37:3, pp. 571–8, p. 571.

31. Ibid, p. 575.

32. Sen, 'Population', p. 462.

33. Ibid.

34. Martin Fritz and Max Koch, 'Economic development and prosperity patterns around the world: Structural challenges for a global steady-state economy', *Global Environmental Change*, 2016, 38, pp. 41–8, p. 41.

35. Ibid.

36. Steffen et al., 'The Anthropocene', p. 740.

37. Judith Stephenson, Karen Newman, and Susannah Mayhew, 'Population dynamics and climate change: What are the links?' *Journal of Public Health*, 2010, 32:2, pp. 150–6, p. 151.

38. Ibid, p. 151.

39. Ibid, p. 154.
40. Steffen et al., 'The Anthropocene', p. 739.
41. Ibid, p. 743.
42. Ibid, p. 746.
43. Ibid, p. 746.
44. Stephenson et al., 'Population dynamics', p. 150.
45. Steffen et al., 'The Anthropocene', p. 741.
46. Fritz and Koch, 'Economic development', p. 41.
47. Ibid, p. 43.
48. Fritz and Koch, 'Economic development', p. 43.
49. Ibid.
50. Ibid, p. 44.
51. Ibid.
52. Ibid, p. 46.
53. Ibid, p. 47.
54. Glen Peters, Jan Minx, Christopher Weber and Ottman Edenhofer, 'Growth in emission transfers via international trade from 1990 to 2008', *PNAS,* 2011, 108:21, pp. 8903–8, p. 8903.
55. Peters et al., 'Growth in emissions', p. 8095.
56. Ibid, p. 8907.
57. Stephenson et al., 'Population dynamics', p. 154.
58. Raphael Billé, Renaud Lapeyre and Romain Porard, 'Biodiversity conservation and poverty alleviation: a way out of the deadlock?' *S.A.P.I.E.N.S.: Surveys and Perspectives Intergrating Environment and Society,* 2012, 5:1 sapiens.revues.org/1452. Accessed 28 April 2016.
59. Steffen et al., 'The Anthropocene', p. 747.
60. Sean McDonagh, *On Care for Our Common Home,* p. 53.
61. Billé et al., 'Biodiversity conservation'.
62. Ibid.
63. Sean McDonagh, *On Care for Our Common Home,* p. 65.
64. Billé et al., 'Biodiversity conservation' p. 12.
65. Ibid.
66. Ibid.
67. Ibid.
68. European Commission, 'Closing the loop: Commission adopts ambitious new Circular Economy Package to boost competitiveness, create jobs and generate sustainable growth', *European Commission Press Release Database,* 2 December 2015, europa.eu/rapid/press-release_IP-15-6203_en.htm
69. Billé et al., 'Biodiversity conservation', p. 12.
70. Ibid.
71. Ibid.
72. Stephenson et al., 'Population dynamics,' p. 150.
73. Billé et al., 'Biodiversity conservation'.
74. Elinor Ostrom, 'A General Framework for Analysing Sustainability of Social-Ecological Systems', *Science,* 2009, 5939, pp. 419–22.
75. Fritz and Koch, 'Economic development', p. 47.
76. Michael Thompson, 'Visions of the Future' in Ruesen, Jörn Fehr, Michael and Thomas Rieger, *Thinking Utopia: Stepping Into Other Worlds,* New York: Berghahn, 2005, pp. 32–52, p. 41.

List of Contributors

Donal Dorr is a theologian and a member of St Patrick's Missionary Society. He has lived and worked as a missionary in several African countries. He is the author of ten books, mainly on issues of spirituality and international social justice, including *Option for the Poor and for the Earth: From Leo XIII to Pope Francis*, (Orbis Books, 2016).

John Feehan was a senior lecturer at University College Dublin. He has written extensively on the natural and cultural heritage of the Irish landscape and many broader aspects of environmental species and theology. His publications include: *The Singing Heart of the World: Creation, Evolution and Faith* (Columba Press, 2010), *Farming in Ireland: History, Heritage and Environment* (UCD, 2003) and *The Landscape of Slieve Bloom* (Blackwater Press, 1979).

Lorna Gold is vice chair of the Global Catholic Climate Movement, which came about to promote *Laudato Si'* across the world. She has worked with Trócaire on matters of Irish climate policy and action for over a decade. Gold writes and speaks extensively on climate justice, ecology and spirituality.

Seán Healy is an SMA priest and **Brigid Reynolds** is a Marist sister. They are both directors of Social Justice Ireland. For more than thirty years they have been active on issues of socio-economic policy in Ireland. Before that they both worked for more than ten years in Africa. Seán Healy and Brigid Reynolds have written or edited more than thirty books on public policy and three books on spirituality and social engagement. Their most recent publication was *A New Social Contract for a New Century: Securing Solidarity and the Common Good* and was published in April 2017.

Peader Kirby is professor emeritus of international politics and public policy at the University of Limerick. His latest book, written with Tadhg O'Mahony, is *The Political Economy of the Low-Carbon Transition: Pathways Beyond Techno-Optimism* (Palgrave Macmillan, 2017). Kirby is chair of the board of Sustainable Projects Ireland, the charity that established and manages Cloughjordan Ecovillage, where he lives.

Dermot A. Lane is parish priest of Balally and former president of Mater Dei Institute of Education, Dublin City University. He is author of *Stepping Stones to Other Religions: A Christian Theology of Interreligious Dialogue* (Veritas, 2011/Orbis, 2012) and editor of *Vatican II in Ireland, Fifty Years On* (Peter Lang, 2015).

Michael Punch is a volunteer in Gardiner Street Church, where he contributes as a reader. He is a former lecturer in sociology in UCD, but a serious accident forced him to retire disabled. Most recently he has completed an MA with the Spirituality Institute for Research and Education.

Cathriona Russell is assistant professor of theology at Trinity College Dublin. Her research interests include theological perspective in environmental ethics and hermeneutics, science and religion, theological anthropology, research ethics and medical ethics. Her most recent book is *Ethics for Graduate Researchers: A Cross-Disciplinary Approach*, which she edited with Linda Hogan and Maureen Junker-Kenny (Elsevier, 2013).

John Sweeney is a climate scientist who has worked on climate change issues for almost forty years as professor emeritus at Maynooth University and has over a hundred publications on this and related topics. He has been a contributing author and review editor to the Intergovernmental Panel on Climate Change Fourth Assessment Report. Sweeney has attended both COP21 in Paris and the launch of *Laudato Si'* in Rome.